The Guide to

West Coast Cheese

The Guide to

West Coast Cheese

MORE THAN 300 CHEESES HANDCRAFTED IN CALIFORNIA, OREGON, AND WASHINGTON

Sasha Davies

TIMBER PRESS
PORTLAND • LONDON

To my husband, Michael,
without whom my life in cheese
and so many other wonderful things
would not be possible.

Photographs by the author. Illustrations by Rory Phillips.
Design by Jane jeszeck/Jigsaw, www.jigsawseattle.com
Maps by Jason Clark of Clark Cartography.
Cheese labels are used with permission from each company.
Frontispiece: *A stack of Rinconada Dairy cheeses on display at Raymond & Co. Cheesemongers in Glen Ellen, California*

Published in 2010 by Timber Press, Inc.

The Haseltine Building
133 S.W. Second Avenue, Suite 450
Portland, Oregon 97204-3527
www.timberpress.com

2 The Quadrant
135 Salusbury Road
London NW6 6RJ
www.timberpress.co.uk

ISBN-13: 978-1-60469-090-3

Printed in China

Library of Congress Cataloging-in-Publication Data

Davies, Sasha.
The guide to West Coast cheese : more than 300 cheeses handcrafted in California, Oregon, and Washington / Sasha Davies.
p. cm.
Includes bibliographical references and index.
ISBN 978-1-60469-090-3
1. Cheese—Pacific Coast (U.S.)—Guidebooks. 2. Cheese—Varieties—Pacific Coast (U.S.)—Guidebooks. 3. Cheesemakers—Pacific Coast (U.S.)—Guidebooks. I. Title.
SF274.U6D393 2010
641.3'730979—dc22

2009053733

Contents

MAPS 6

ACKNOWLEDGMENTS 9

PREFACE 10

A BRIEF HISTORY OF WEST COAST CHEESEMAKING 12

CHEESE FROM FARM TO TABLE 15

CHEESE TYPES 28

CHEESE AT HOME 49

CHEESE ATLAS 55

CHEESEMAKERS 206

SHOPS 210

GLOSSARY 213

BIBLIOGRAPHY 215

WEST COAST CHEESE BY TYPE 216

INDEX 219

Color photographs begin on page 33.

Washington Cheesemakers

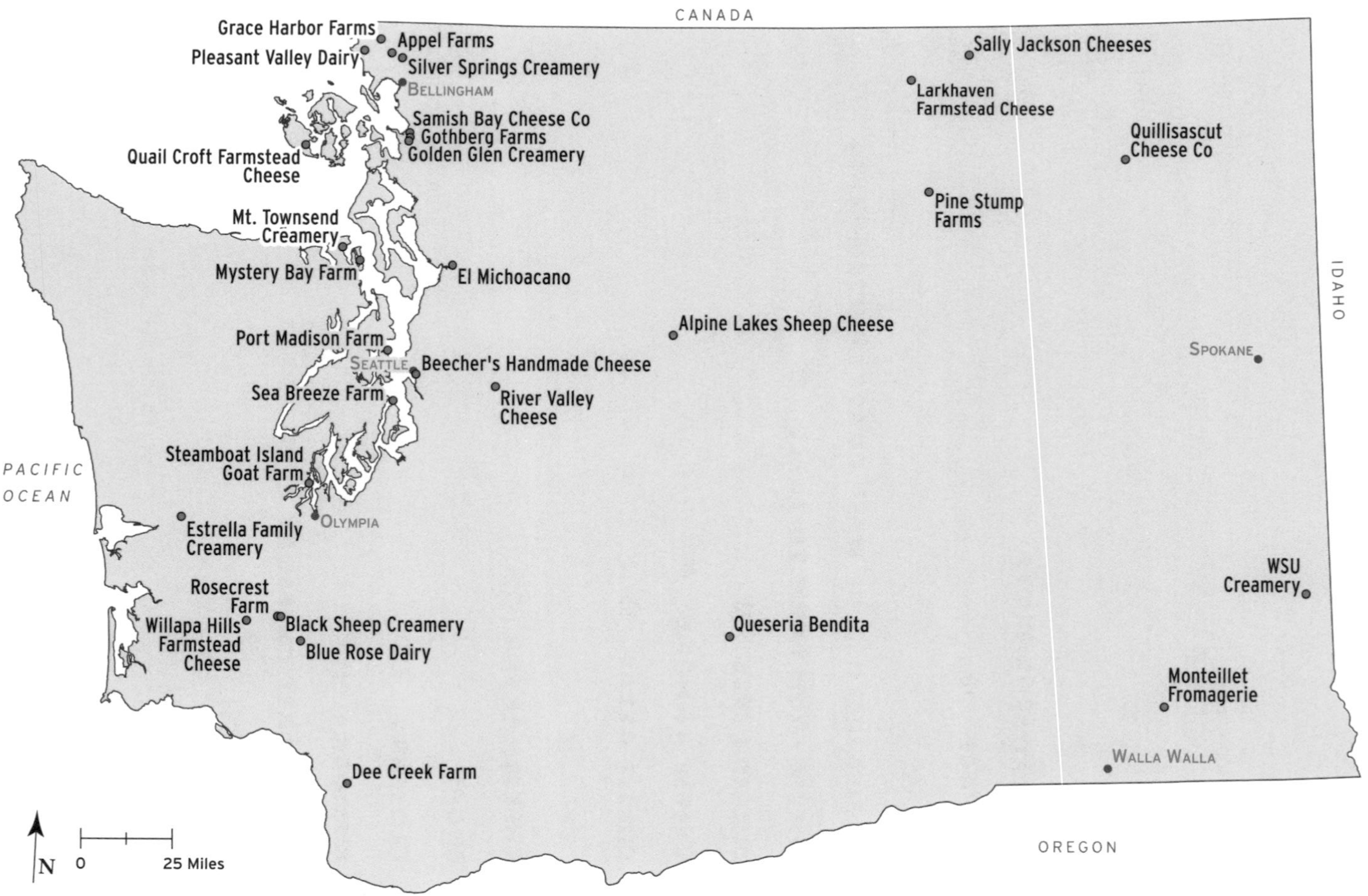

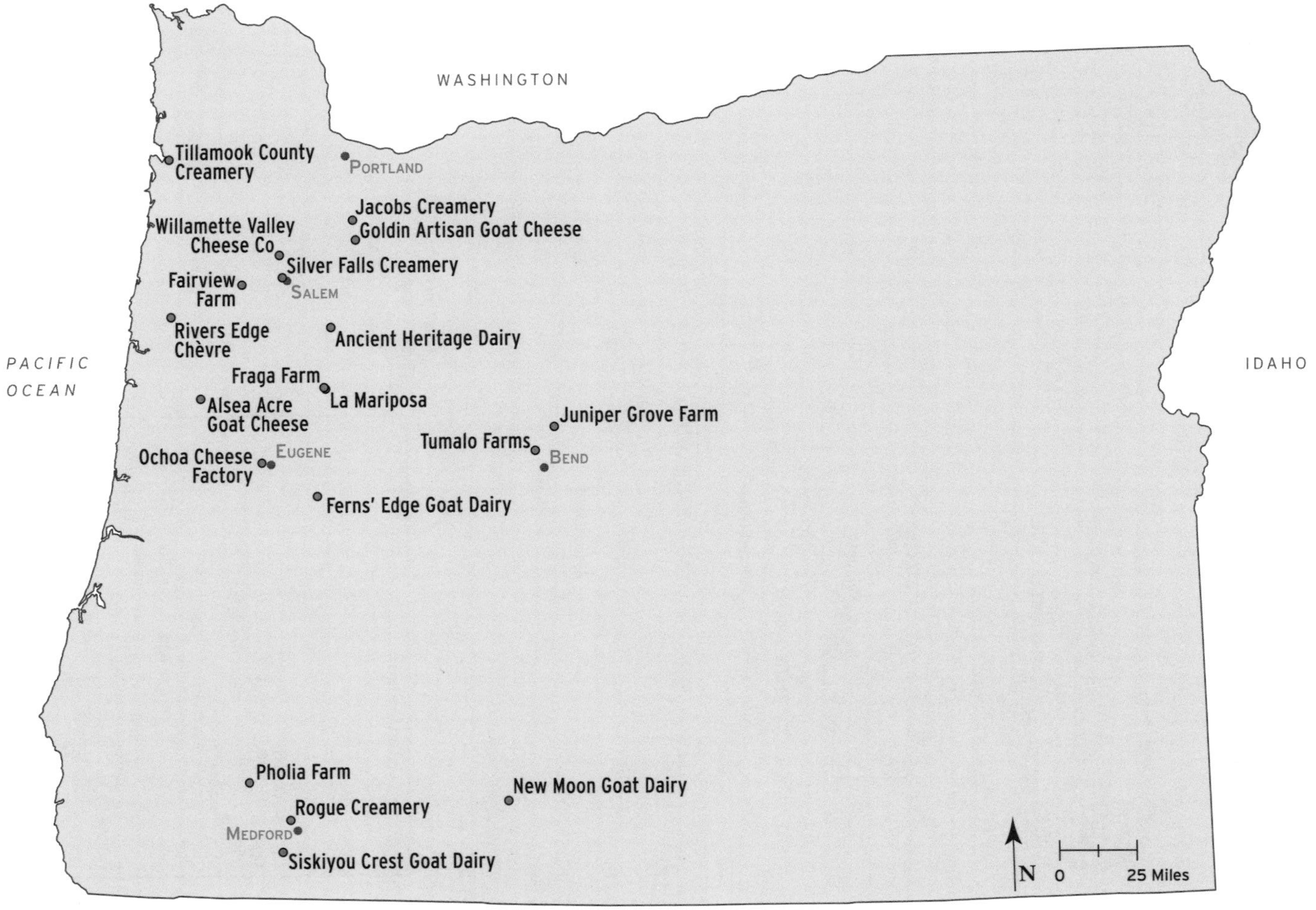

Oregon Cheesemakers

California Cheesemakers
OREGON
NEVADA
ARIZONA
MEXICO
PACIFIC OCEAN
Rumiano Cheese Co
Cypress Grove Chevre
Eureka
Loleta Cheese Factory
Redding
North Valley Farms Chevre
Pedrozo Dairy & Cheese Co
Sierra Nevada Cheese Co
Shamrock Artisan Goat Cheese
Yerba Santa Goat Dairy
La Clarine Farm
Sacramento
See inset
Fiscalini Farmstead Cheese Co
Belfiore Cheese Co
San Francisco
Oakdale Cheese
Central Coast Creamery
Modesto
Nicolau Farms
Meyenberg Goat Milk Products
Harley Farms
Midcoast Cheese Co
Bravo Farms
Three Sisters Farmstead Cheese
Kendall Farms
Bakersfield
Rinconada Dairy
Los Angeles
Gioia Cheese Co
Bubalus Bubalis
Winchester Cheese Co
San Diego
N
0
100 Miles
Pug's Leap Farm
Healdsburg
Goat's Leap
Redwood Hill Farm
Santa Rosa
Bohemian Creamery
Matos Cheese Factory
Bodega Artisan Cheese
Valley Ford Cheese
Delice de la Vallee
Bellwether Farms
Two Rock Valley
Vella Cheese Co
Sonoma
Napa
Spring Hill Cheese Co
Cowgirl Creamery
Achadinha Cheese Co
Petaluma
Laura Chenel's Chevre
Andante Dairy
Barinaga Ranch
Marin French Cheese Co
Point Reyes Farmstead Cheese Co
0
10 Miles

Acknowledgments

I would like to thank all the people who have offered their generous help and support to make this book a reality.

First and foremost, I extend my deepest gratitude to the cheesemakers of California, Oregon, and Washington not only for the wonderful cheeses they produce but also for the time they dedicated to assist me with this book.

A special thanks to Alyce Birchenough, Allison Hooper, and Paula Lambert; women who have made incredible contributions to the greater world of American cheese, encouraged all of my endeavors in the industry, and provided endless technical information on cheese and cheesemaking.

Tami Parr, Kim Iannotti, Steve Jones, and Lynne Devereaux are cheese colleagues that I am lucky enough to call my friends. They have provided logistical support, cheese samples, and encouragement throughout the creation of this guide.

With immense gratitude for time they spent reviewing pieces of the manuscript and their constructive criticisms, I'd like to thank Bryan Davies, Rose Gabaeff, and Jonathan Tepperman.

Last but not least, a heartfelt thank you to my editor, Mollie Firestone, for her meticulous work on this book from start to finish, and to the folks at Timber Press for rallying behind the West Coast Cheese movement.

Preface

The very first cheesemaker I visited after I began working in the industry was California's Cowgirl Creamery. My father and I drove out to Point Reyes Station to watch cheesemaker Maureen Cunnie make Red Hawk—a washed rind gem perfectly suited to the damp, coastal climate. Through the viewing window we could see Maureen and her team scoop small, silken cubes of curds into the drum-shaped forms. Whey rushed down the gently sloped table, draining off one corner into a tall bucket. Rolling racks of Red Hawk and Mt. Tam, stacked almost as high as the ceiling, were shuffled around to make room for incoming cheese. I was intoxicated by the aromas, the process, and even the tidy uniforms, stark white all the way down to the squeaky rubber boots. There was no turning back.

It took a couple of years for my attention to stretch beyond the cheeses themselves: all I wanted to do was look at them, taste them, and learn how they were made. When my palate was somewhat sated, I started to think more about the origin of each cheese, specifically the land and people behind it. Embarking on an adventurous project called Cheese by Hand, my husband and I began a four-month road trip around the United States with scheduled visits to forty small-scale cheesemakers. I met with West Coast leaders in the American cheese movement who have created some of the most iconic of U.S. cheeses, such as Humboldt Fog from Cypress Grove Chevre and Rogue River Blue from Rogue Creamery. I learned that they do so much more than just making wonderful cheeses. Each has been a fixture within their community for decades, providing jobs and fostering growth and stability for regional dairy farms. Something clicked for me at this point and I understood that cheese is more than a delectable food: it's a vehicle for community and for understanding our relationship to the land.

Even with this more pragmatic perspective, I am still moved by the romantic side of cheese and the rustic treasures that can be found by rumbling down dusty, unpaved roads and following hand-painted signs. Walking through the door of the Matos Cheese Factory in northern California is like stepping back in time. On the simple countertop sits an old cash register and a mesh-covered cut wheel of St. George, the only cheese they make. The stark white walls are adorned with a cross and a couple of tea towels displaying maps of the Azores, the homeland of the Matos family. The open door behind the counter offers a peek at ceiling-height shelves filled with golden rounds, each one marked with a date in red pen.

When I was first learning about cheese, two of my favorite books were reference-style guides that profiled individual cheeses from specific regions. These were invaluable in helping me to understand what to expect from each cheese and arming me with useful details such as seasonality and pairing suggestions. After relocating from New York to Oregon, I searched for ways to discover the intimate details of the astounding bounty of cheese in the western states. Those guides, coupled with my burning desire to know more about West Coast cheeses, were the inspiration for this project.

This book is written for cheese-curious consumers at any level: beginning, expert, and everything in between. The first several chapters contain primers on dairy animals, cheesemaking, and enjoying cheese at home; these represent the highlights of what I've learned in classes, with cheesemakers, from books, and alongside the many experts I've worked for in the industry. What follows is the Cheese Atlas, which details more than 300 cheeses that are made in California, Oregon, and Washington. Woven throughout the cheese entries are more in-depth explorations of some commonly produced cheeses, as well as profiles of specific producers who are not only making beautiful cheese but are also taking an innovative approach to their work. In the back of the book you will find resources to help further your cheese experience: a glossary of helpful terms, a list of the cheesemakers included in this guide, and a selection of U.S. shops that stock West Coast cheese.

I hope you all enjoy tasting your way through this book as much as I have!

A Brief History of West Coast Cheesemaking

Welcome to the world of West Coast cheese. Since the mid-1990s specialty cheesemaking has seen staggering growth in California, Oregon, and Washington. The copious lists of new cheeses and articles about the growing number of creameries clearly indicate that this region is experiencing a cheese renaissance.

As with other areas of the country, agriculture out West was mostly a regional affair until the rise of industrial production around the time of World War II. The development of refrigeration, followed by improvements in transportation supported the shift toward factory production. These early facilities were closer to cooperatives, with regional dairy farms pooling milk in one location for bottling and cheese production. After World War II things began to change; California, Oregon, and Washington began to lose small dairy farms and cooperative creameries. These were often replaced by the industrial dairies and cheese plants that are now widespread.

In the 1970s, a back-to-the-land movement began in the western states that aimed to slow the growth of industrial agriculture. The abundance of local cheeses and farms that we see today is a direct result of the hard work and determination of members of that small revolution who were interested in reacquainting themselves with the origin of the food they consumed.

The successful rebirth of dairies in California, Oregon, and Washington is also, at least partially, due to each of these coastal states having the temperate climate and sizeable areas of broad, grass-growing landscape to support dairying. Add to this a wealth of hard-working immigrants, many from nations such as Holland, France, and Italy with impressive fresh and aged cheeses, and you have the makings for a strong dairy industry.

Having been around for thousands of years, cheese itself is not new to us. But our understanding of it as an agricultural product that directly involves land, animals, and people is being renewed. Keep all of these contributors in mind as you explore and enjoy the bounty of cheeses produced on the West Coast.

CALIFORNIA

California's fertile landscape, and the wealth of geographies and climates within its borders, have made it into an agricultural juggernaut. But these gifts haven't come without a cost. The physical beauty and appealing climate of California continues to attract floods of new residents, forcing the state to balance agriculture and development. This has hugely affected dairies, as rising land prices have forced many farmers to leave the state or to do more with less land, which usually means shifting from a pasture-based to a confinement operation.

While there aren't many regional dairies remaining, Marin French Cheese Company, Rumiano Cheese Company, and Vella Cheese Company have over 300 years of combined experience producing handcrafted cheeses. In the 1970s they were joined by Laura Chenel's Chevre and Redwood Hill Farm, goat cheese producers who helped introduce America to fresh chèvre. A handful of back-to-the-landers followed, such as Cypress Grove Chevre and Bodega Artisan Cheese.

Consumers in California have supported the growth of many more small-scale cheese producers and the state's milk advisory board has educated cow dairy owners about cheesemaking in hopes of helping them add value to their milk during tough economic times. The development of larger scale specialty cheese producers in California has led to a slightly contentious split in the cheese community between independent, small-scale producers and larger producers.

OREGON

As recently as the 1960s, the last of the local creameries still dotted Oregon's coast. Each region had a creamery—fed with milk from local dairies—that sold butter, fresh milk and cream, and cheese. As the dairy economies dwindled, timber businesses developed, and agriculture industrialized, these creameries gradually shut down and larger cooperatives were formed. Among the most well-known, farmer-owned cooperatives to emerge from this shift is Tillamook County Creamery. Tillamook is an anchor in Oregon's dairy industry, producing Cheddar cheese for just over one hundred years with milk from farms surrounding the creamery on northern Oregon's rugged coastline.

At the southern end of the state is Rogue Creamery, a cheesemaking facility which has been in operation since 1935. During World War II the founder of California's Vella Cheese Company, Tom Vella, saw an opportunity to create food that could make the journey overseas to feed troops. With backing from J. L. Kraft, Vella began producing block Cheddar cheese at the Rogue Creamery's Central Point facility.

Since the late 1990s, the back-to-the-land contingent and others interested in smaller scale food production have developed cheese operations throughout the state. Many producers consider Oregon to be a friendly state for cheesemakers as there is great support from the Dairy Farmers of Oregon and a general enthusiasm toward independent businesses.

WASHINGTON

Similar to Oregon, Washington has a wonderful landscape and climate for cow dairies along its coast. Whatcom county, the northernmost on Washington's western coastline, contains the largest concentration of dairies in the state. The hardscrabble land of the far eastern part of the state is better suited to goats and sheep.

Washington is home to many of the contributing farms and the headquarters of Darigold, one of the nation's largest milk processors. Darigold evolved from the United Dairymen's Association, a handful of cooperatives who came together in the early 1900s to collectively market their milk and dairy products. Washington State University has also been experimenting with and producing cheese since the turn of the twentieth century. They are well known for the development of cheese packaged in tins, popular at the time because of its ability to withstand contamination and the stresses of transportation.

In the late 1960s and early 1970s, resisting the industrialization of their food, Sally Jackson (Sally Jackson Cheeses) and George Train (Pleasant Valley Dairy) each started farmstead creameries on opposite sides of the state and began producing regional cheeses. The majority of Washington's smaller scale producers have emerged since the late 1990s, possibly encouraged by the interest of local food consumers. A steady increase in the number of farmers' markets has helped reduce the entry barrier into the retail marketplace as well as educating residents about the food produced in their own local area and state.

Cheese from Farm to Table

Dairy farms are the first link in the cheesemaking chain because they are the source of the most essential ingredient. Milk is truly one of nature's miracles—food that a mammalian mother can provide for her young. Just like humans, cows, goats, and sheep must give birth in order to produce milk. Millions of young are born to dairy animals each year to kick off the milk production (lactation) cycle. Most of these young are sold for meat, having fulfilled their usefulness on the farm by enabling their mothers to produce milk.

People often wonder why dairy animals can't be milked indefinitely once they give birth. Many human mothers nurse their children for years, and while this could be done with dairy animals (and sometimes is) it is not the most productive scenario for cheesemaking. Mammal lactation cycles are designed to provide their young with maximum nourishment at birth and then gradually decline in volume and nutrients over time. The natural progression is for the suckling young to expand their diet beyond their mother's milk. So the longer a dairy animal is milked, the lower the volume and components (the ratio of solids—fats, proteins, and minerals—to water) of the milk. This ultimately means less cheese for the cheesemaker.

Complex flavors come from carefully produced and handled milk so exceptional cheese cannot be made with mediocre or low-quality milk. Cheese only has three other ingredients: salt, cultures, and coagulants. While all ingredients are big contributors to the development of the cheese, milk makes up the volume. Think of it this way: flour is to bread what milk is to cheese—the bulk of the ingredients and a serious influence on the flavor and texture of the end product.

SELECTING MILK FOR CHEESEMAKING

When cheesemakers evaluate milk they are interested in three things: flavor, the volume of milk, and the components of the milk. Volume and components vary greatly across animal types and among breeds within animal types. If you've tasted cow, goat, and sheep cheeses, you know that each has a unique flavor.

To complicate matters a bit, the components and flavor of the milk are affected by the animal's diet and the length of milking time. Milk from animals raised on pasture will have more variability because pastures are often quite diverse and change regularly with the seasons. Strictly grass-fed animals will not produce as much milk as those supplemented with grain and the milk produced will taste different too.

Cheesemakers might begin by selecting an animal type and then evaluate breeds to see which best suits their needs.

Popular Cow Breeds

Holsteins have the highest volume of milk of all dairy cows and a lower fat content than all other common breeds.

Brown Swiss are second to Holsteins in milk volume. They are well-adapted to harsh climates.

Jerseys are smaller animals that produce high-fat content milk.

Ayrshires are well-adapted to rocky farms and harsh winters.

Guernseys are smaller animals known for their docile temperament and the rich flavor of their milk.

Popular Goat Breeds

Nubians produce high-quality, high-butterfat milk.

Alpines are good milkers, adaptable to many climates, and have long lactation cycles.

LaManchas are strong, hardy, and well-suited to northern climates and conditions.

Saanen do well in a variety of climates and produce record-high milk volumes.

Popular Sheep Breeds

East Friesians are the most popular and have the highest milk volume of sheep in the United States.

Lacaunes have slightly more total solids in milk but lower volume than East Friesians.

Seasonal Cheesemaking

The term *seasonal* can indicate that a cheesemaker only makes cheese during a specific part of the year. This time of year is often when the animals can be out on pasture. Cheesemakers do this because they feel that their cheese benefits from milk produced while the animals are feeding on grass or available forage. Feed has a tremendous impact on the components and flavors in milk, including fat, protein, and mineral contents.

Seasonal can also mean that animals are milked only in a specific season or time of year, rather than year-round. If breeding is seasonal, meaning that the animals are kept to the same birthing and lactation cycle, then cheesemaking would stop for two to four months out of the year, depending on the animal type, because the animals would go dry in the weeks prior to giving birth.

Average Milk Yields

One of the most frequently asked questions about cheese is exactly how much milk is needed to make it. The yield, or final cheese poundage, varies greatly depending on the style of cheese being made. For example, the same amount of milk will have a higher yield when making fresh, high-moisture cheese, as compared to hard cheese in which as much moisture as possible has been pressed from the curds.

The three diagrams that follow illustrate the average milk yields for cows, goats, and sheep. The first calculation in each diagram shows the amount of milk produced in one day and how much cheese that milk could produce. The second calculation shows how much milk each animal type requires to make a single pound of cheese. Commercial and small-scale cheesemakers measure milk by weight (in pounds) so each diagram also shows the ratio of pounds to gallons.

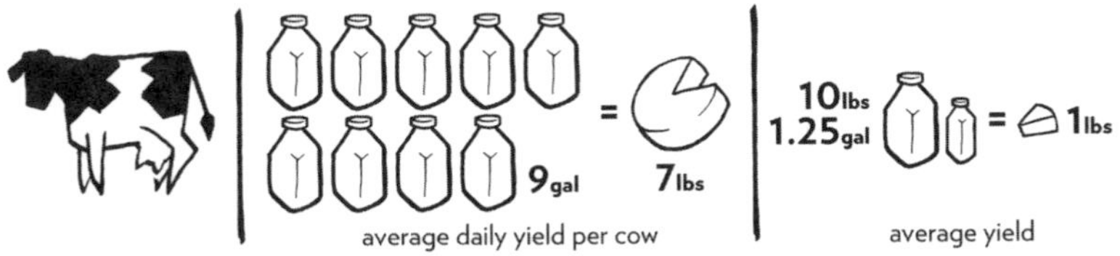

Cows have the highest milk production but also have the lowest yield.

Goats produce much less milk than cows but have a better yield of cheese.

Sheep have the lowest milk production and the highest yield.

FARMSTEAD OR CREAMERY

The way milk is produced dramatically affects its flavor and components. When producing milk for cheesemaking, a dairy farmer has to think about pasture management, weather fluctuations, animal comfort, feed, genetics, and even urban encroachment. Some cheesemakers opt for complete control from the production of the milk through the aging of the cheese while others decide to focus exclusively on cheese production and purchase their milk from a dairy farm.

Farmstead operations refer to cheesemakers who use milk from their own herd on the same land where they make the cheese. This term is often associated with bucolic images of red barns, milk cans, and twenty cow dairies, but it is actually not a good indicator of an operation's size or its farming practices. Within the farmstead category there are confinement operations, grazing operations with animals on pasture 365 days a year, and everything in between. Creameries operate by purchasing milk from a dairy farm rather than having a herd on site. While creamery owners do not have the burden of managing a herd of dairy animals, they do have to track down adequate amounts of milk that is of high enough quality for cheesemaking. It can be difficult to find dairy farmers who are willing to alter their feed management style, or breed, in order to produce the best milk for cheesemaking.

HERD MANAGEMENT METHODS

Dairy farms can manage the housing and feed of their animals in a variety of ways. Pasture-based and confinement are two herd management methods. An operation may stick with a single method or create a hybrid system depending on the available resources.

In a pasture-based system animals feed on pasture whenever possible. Pasture conditions vary greatly from farm-to-farm depending on geography, climate, available space, the market value of the land surrounding a farm, and even state regulations. For example, dairy farmers in Washington are prohibited from grazing their animals during heavy rains. So, often even pasture-based farms may keep their animals in confinement for some part of the year. The majority of pasture-based dairies feed the animals some portion of grain during milking.

Confinement refers to keeping animals within the confines of a barn, loafing shed, or other form of penned-in area. Loafing areas (pasture, dirt, or concrete) are often available so animals can move around freely when they are not being milked. Confinement systems evolved because they were considered more efficient given that the farmer no longer had to move animals around, or maintain fences and water supply lines. Animals kept in confinement can be fed any combination of a total mixed ration (TMR), dry forage (such as hay or alfalfa), silage (fermented forage), and grain.

CERTIFICATIONS

In addition to distinctions such as farmstead or creamery, cheesemakers can pursue a number of certifications to help consumers understand the principles and practices of their operation. Certifications usually have some cost associated with them, such as the cost of making adjustments to meet set standards or the cost of having an audit completed.

It is important to remember that certifications are optional. While the presence of a certification validates specific practices and principles of the producers that have it, the absence of a certification does not necessarily mean that a producer is not maintaining the same practices or principles.

ANIMAL WELFARE APPROVED. Certifies that animals on a farm are able to behave naturally and have physical and psychological well-being. This program is only available to independent family farms. Free. www.animalwelfareapproved.org.

CERTIFIED HUMANE RAISED AND HANDLED. Evaluates treatment of animals from birth through death, and prohibits use of antibiotics or hormones. Fee-based. www.certifiedhumane.org.

CERTIFIED ORGANIC. Standards are set at the federal level by The Organic Food Production Act of 1990 and the National Organic Program. Fee-based. www.ams.usda.gov/nop/.

FOOD ALLIANCE SUSTAINABLE PRODUCER. This certification focuses on sustainability while examining environment, animal welfare, labor practices, and consumer affairs. Fee-based. www.foodalliance.org.

KOSHER. Certifies that a cheese and its production conform to rules of the Jewish religion. Fee-based.

VALIDUS CERTIFIED RESPONSIBLE PRODUCER. Evaluates standards in animal welfare, environmental impact, and on-farm security (animal traceability, disease prevention). Fee-based. www.validuscertified.com.

OTHER KEY INGREDIENTS

Although milk is the primary ingredient in cheese, salt, cultures, and coagulants play a critical role in the cheesemaking process. Each ingredient has a unique influence on the development of a cheese's flavor and texture.

Salt

Salt is an especially valuable tool for cheesemakers. A cheesemaker can use salt to help extract moisture from curds or freshly formed wheels of cheese. (Think about what happens to an eggplant when you sprinkle salt on it.) Salt can also be used to discourage the growth of specific bacteria or molds on the outside of the cheese or to create the ideal environment for a particular yeast or mold, enabling cheesemakers to cultivate the type of rind they want. In addition, salt is used in cheese to add flavor, just as it might be used in your kitchen.

Cultures

Cultures are the most overlooked ingredients in cheese, at least by cheese consumers. Cultures directly influence what happens in the vat where the cheese is made and also the development of flavors and textures during aging. Once a cheesemaker knows what style of cheese they are interested in making they often consult with a culture supplier to determine the best culture or cultures to achieve the desired result.

Cultures are divided into two groups: starter and secondary. Starter cultures, as the name implies, are used at the beginning of the cheesemaking process to ripen the milk. These cultures are groups of bacteria that feed on lactose, the naturally occurring sugar in milk. The bacteria convert lactose to lactic acid, which increases the overall acidity of the milk and creates an ideal environment for coagulation, the next step in cheesemaking. Secondary cultures, often a combination of yeasts, molds, and bacteria, are selected to perform specialized tasks, such as the development of a variety of rinds or the development of the eyes (holes) in Swiss cheese. The secondary cultures can be added to the milk alongside starter cultures at the beginning of the cheesemaking process or applied to the surface of newly formed cheeses.

Coagulants

Coagulants are responsible for accelerating the natural process of milk solids (proteins and fats) joining together to form curds. Although milk will form curds on its own if left in a warm spot for a long enough period of time (something many of us have experienced in our own kitchens), most cheesemakers add either an animal, microbial, or plant coagulant.

Two reasons dictate why cheesemakers choose to add coagulants (rapid coagulation) instead of allowing the milk to transform into cheese in its own time (lactic coagulation). First of all, the body or structure of curds that develop during lactic coagulation are not as sturdy as those that are helped along by a coagulant. Secondly, lactic coagulation creates more acidity than is desired for many cheese types. Coagulation can be described along a continuum from lactic to rapid because many cheeses are made with a combination of the two methods. When a cheese is made primarily by lactic coagulation this means that very little coagulant was added.

When selecting a coagulant, a cheesemaker considers its effectiveness, the impact it will have on flavor development, and also whether the coagulant is considered vegetarian.

ANIMAL RENNET. Also called traditional rennet, this is made of an enzyme found in one of the stomachs of a suckling calf, kid, or lamb. The enzyme is important for these young ruminant animals because their diet for the first couple months of their lives is strictly milk. Rennet enables the solids in milk to separate from the liquids and band together in clumps. Solids take longer to pass through the young animal's system, which allows their body to extract the maximum amount of nutrients from the milk.

Rennet is extracted in a number of different ways, sometimes by soaking dehydrated pieces of the stomach in liquid and sometimes by extracting a small portion of the enzyme from the animal's stomach and propagating it in a lab. Cheesemakers used to make their own rennet by soaking the stomachs in water or whey, thereby creating a liquid solution that they could add to the milk (rather than dropping a small piece of the stomach into the cheese vat). Today most cheesemakers purchase rennet in either dissolvable tablets or a concentrated liquid solution.

MICROBIAL COAGULANT. All microbial coagulants are produced through fermentation. Select bacteria are grown on a medium in a lab and a byproduct of the bacterial activity is the coagulant. The lab then separates the bacteria so that they collect pure coagulant.

There are two types of microbial coagulants. The first is a yeast culture that has had a gene from a calf spliced into it. Because the yeast carries that calf gene, when the yeast develops it produces the exact same enzyme produced by the calf's stomach. The second type of microbial coagulant is fermented from a mold spore. When fermented, this spore makes an enzyme that works like rennet. The mold spore coagulant once had a reputation for bitter flavors in cheese, but a lot of work has gone into improving the purity of the spore to produce a cleaner enzyme with fewer taste issues.

While both of these microbial coagulants are considered vegetarian by cheesemakers, some would argue that the yeast culture, while not coming directly from an animal, is still a derivative animal product. Others might say that there is no such thing as vegetarian cheese.

PLANT COAGULANT. Thistles are the most commonly used plant coagulant. The main drawback to using them is that they contain a number of other enzymes that contribute additional flavors that may or may not be desirable. Plant coagulants are not often utilized in the United States.

Thistle plant used as coagulant

THE CHEESEMAKING PROCESS

Prior to starting to make the cheese, the producer must decide whether to pasteurize the milk. Pasteurization is the process of heating milk to a temperature hot enough to kill bacteria. This process originated as a method to eliminate risks posed by harmful bacteria that can contaminate milk and also in hopes of extending the shelf life of milk.

Pasteurization, also known as High Temperature Short Hold (HTSH), requires milk to be heated to 161 degrees F and held for fifteen to twenty seconds. A milder form of pasteurization called heat treatment or Low Temperature Long Hold (LTLH) requires the milk to be heated to 145 degrees F and held for at least thirty minutes. The lower the heat, the lower the impact on bacteria in the milk that might foster flavor and texture development.

Raw milk (also referred to as unpasteurized) does not undergo any form of heat treatment so all naturally occurring bacteria remain in the milk when cheesemaking begins. FDA legislation in the United States dictates that any cheese made from raw milk must be aged for a minimum of sixty days because that was determined to be the point at which most harmful bacteria could not longer survive within a cheese.

While there is great debate over the relative potential of raw and pasteurized milk to produce ranges of flavors and textures in cheese, the most important thing to remember is that cheese can be made safely from both types of milk by anyone with sound sanitation practices.

Cheesemaking Steps

There are ten basic cheesemaking steps though each one is not required to make every variety of cheese. For example, when making chèvre the curds could be bagged or ladled into forms after the first two steps, and a Camembert-style cheese would only require steps one through five plus time for draining and aging. It is helpful to look at these steps as the building blocks available to cheesemakers; they will select the blocks they need to build the specific cheese they are making.

STEP 1: RIPENING THE MILK. Starter cultures are added to the milk and convert lactose to lactic acid. Often the milk will be heated slightly to create an optimal environment for starter cultures to rapidly grow and reproduce.

STEP 2: COAGULATING. One type of coagulant (animal, microbial, or plant) is added to the milk. This begins the process of curd formation as solids (proteins and fats) are pulled away from the water and encouraged to knit together.

STEP 3: ADDING SECONDARY CULTURES. Type-specific cultures and/or molds are added. These will affect everything from flavor development to the type of rind that grows.

STEP 4: CUTTING THE CURD. Cutting through the gentle flan-like mass allows the solids (curds) to release liquid (whey). The size that the curds are cut to depends on the style of cheese being made. The smaller the curds are cut the harder the cheese will be (low-moisture cheeses like Parmigiano-Reggiano) and the larger the curds are cut, the softer the cheese will be (high-moisture cheeses like Camembert). Curds can be ladled into molds at this point for very soft cheeses like Brie.

STEP 5: HEALING THE CURD. If curds are going to be stirred or heated at all, they will be allowed to rest before proceeding. This allows the curds to shrink and firm up so that they can withstand the movement and heat without falling apart.

STEP 6: COOKING AND/OR WASHING THE CURDS. This is another way for the cheesemaker to continue to expel moisture from the curds and would be done to make a harder cheese. Curds are often stirred vigorously during this step to shrink them and prevent them from clumping together. To cut down the acidity and alter the texture, curds can be washed by draining off some of the whey and replacing it with water. This tends to create a sweeter flavor in the cheese.

STEP 7: WHEYING OFF. The whey is drained out of the vat so that only the curd remains. As with washing, draining removes lactose, which is the food source for acid-producing bacteria. Curds and whey can also be removed from the vat together and poured into forms where the whey will drain off leaving only the curds.

STEP 8: HOOPING. Curds are scooped or pumped out of the vat into their molds or forms. These forms work like colanders by allowing the curds to continue draining. The forms also give the cheeses their shape.

STEP 9: PRESSING/DRAINING. Forms are either stacked one on top of the other or pressed individually beneath weights to continue to expel moisture and encourage curds to fuse together. Cheeses that are not pressed are often left in their forms to allow whey to continue to drain off through gravity alone.

STEP 10: UNHOOPING. Cheeses are removed from their forms and either packaged (fresh cheeses), soaked in a brine tank, or placed in a temperature and humidity controlled environment to begin affinage.

AFFINAGE

Affinage is a French term that describes the aging or curing of cheese. It is during this period of time that flavor and texture development take place. Each cheese has a set of unique requirements for temperature, humidity, and treatments (such as washing, brushing, or turning) that, combined, will ensure its proper development. While affinage cannot fix a bad cheese, it can transform a good cheese into a *great* one.

As a cheese ages, three processes occur: lipolysis, proteolysis, and desiccation. Lipolysis is the breakdown of fats within the cheese. Fats are broken down with the aid of enzymes, altering the texture and flavor of the cheese. Proteolysis is the breakdown of proteins within the cheese and is caused by chain reactions set off by the cultures added to the milk during cheesemaking. Desiccation is a fancy word for loss of moisture. Since bacteria like to live in damp, warmish places, this can be a tricky part of developing cheese recipes. As a cheese ages, it loses moisture and thus becomes a less hospitable environment for bacteria.

Effective curing involves careful orchestration and management of the cheese's conditions so that these things happen at the correct time and rate. A variety of things can be done to alter the development of cheeses, like putting them in a brine (saltwater) solution, rubbing them with dry salt, or washing them with alcohol or brines that contain various bacteria. These treatments, plus a steady regimen of correct temperature and humidity levels, determine what a cheese will become over time whether curing lasts for ten days or eighteen months.

Tyrosine Crystals

Some aged cheeses have small crunchy bits scattered throughout the paste. Rather than salt or anything that the cheesemaker has added, these little bits are naturally formed crystals of the amino acid tyrosine. Amino acids are the building blocks of proteins and some are released during the proteolysis (breakdown of proteins) that happens on the inside of the cheese during aging. Tyrosine becomes solid because it has a low solubility.

Tyrosine crystals always form inside the paste and are not to be confused with Calcium Lactate, another naturally forming crystal. These are the white, powdery crystals that form on the outside of cheeses that are aged in a protective coating and not allowed to develop natural rinds. Both types of crystals are flavorless, but many cheese enthusiasts enjoy them for the texture they add.

Cheese Types

A variety of factors, such as affinage, molds, and treatments, determine the cheese type. Usually the presence of a rind and the texture of the paste (which is everything except the rind) are helpful indicators of the category to which a cheese will belong.

FRESH

Mozzarella

Chèvre

Fresh cheeses have no affinage (or a very brief one) and often have a shorter shelf life than aged cheeses. Generally they do not form a rind and are high in moisture. Many fresh cheeses are made with very little added coagulant. Instead, they rely largely on the work of starter cultures which also have the power to set curd, they just take more time to do it (think hours instead of minutes). Some fresh cheeses involve the step of cutting and washing curds while others are simply poured directly into the form. Common cheeses in this category are chèvre, queso fresco, mozzarella, and fromage blanc.

BLOOMY RIND

Unripe Camembert

Midripe Camembert

Ripe Camembert

Cheeses with a downy, white rind are known as bloomy rinds. The primary mold that develops this bloom is *Penicillium candidum*. There are many strains of *P. candidum*, yielding flavors that range from mild and lactic to ones resembling mushrooms and spring onions. The mold is added to the milk before the coagulant but after the starter bacteria have had a chance to do their job. Because this mold needs oxygen in order to develop, its growth is restricted to the outside of the cheese. Ideal conditions for the growth of *P. candidum* include a surface that is very moist but not wet. Cheesemakers often achieve this by salting the freshly unhooped cheeses. The salting absorbs enough moisture so that the *P. candidum* can get a foothold and bloom, and also discourages the development of any unwanted yeasts or molds. Because of the bacteria growing on the rind, the paste of bloomy rind cheeses breaks down from the outside toward the center. Common cheeses in this category are Camembert, Cirrus, triple creams, and Mt. Tam.

SURFACE-RIPENED

Crottin

Humboldt Fog

Surface-ripened cheeses have a wrinkly looking rind which can be white or cream-colored, and have spots of blue and green molds. They tend to break down a bit right beneath the rind, forming a dense, smooth paste and keeping a chalky or cake-like center. The key ingredient that makes many of these characteristics develop in surface-ripened cheeses is the addition of *Geotrichum candidum*, a yeast that is also used in lower dosages to help with the development of bloomy and washed rind cheeses. Common cheeses in this category are crottin, Inverness, and Legato.

WASHED RIND

Caldwell Crik Chevrette whole

Caldwell Crik Chevrette cut

Stinky is the descriptor most often used for washed rind cheeses. These are exactly what the name implies: cheeses that have their rinds washed. The wash (usually a combination of bacteria, molds, and yeast) encourages the development of *Brevibacterium linens*, the bacteria responsible for imparting orange-brown hues and pungent aromas. Because of the wash, these cheeses ripen primarily from the surface in toward the center and can range in texture from semi-soft all the way to downright runny. Common cheeses in this category are Limburger, Epoisses, Red Hawk, and Caldwell Crik Chevrette.

SEMI-SOFT

Guapier

The unifying characteristic of semi-soft cheeses is their pliable or bendy texture. This texture is achieved in a variety of ways, such as cutting curds into larger pieces so that they retain more moisture, allowing wheels to drain either by gravity or by pressing them only lightly, or sealing the rinds with wax or another protective coating during aging. These cheeses can have natural, waxed, or even washed rinds and can be aged for a couple weeks or a few months. Common cheeses in this category are Colby, jack, Asiago, and Guapier.

SEMI-FIRM

Clothbound Cheddar

Emmental

Semi-firm cheeses tend to have a dense, clay-like, or even slightly crumbly paste. They have less moisture than semi-soft cheeses. The firmer texture of these cheeses is acheived by cutting curds to a smaller size, stirring or cooking curds, and pressing curds when they are first put in their forms. The rinds of semi-firm cheeses can range from natural and rugged with gray and brown molds to oil-rubbed or clothbound. Common cheeses in this category are Emmental, Clothbound Cheddar, and Elk Mountain.

HARD

Aged Pecorino

The key to the texture of hard cheeses is the expulsion of moisture. Less moisture within the cheeses means that they will be able to age considerably longer than other cheeses assuming they are kept in appropriately humid conditions to prevent cracking. In some of these cheeses the curds are also scalded, or cooked, while being stirred to expel even more moisture. Hard cheeses are often brined upon coming out of their hoops, which helps develop the rind, and are sometimes washed with a mixture of brine and bacteria to inhibit the growth of unwanted molds on their surfaces. Common cheeses in this category are Parmigiano-Reggiano, aged pecorino, Mezzo Secco, and Old World Portuguese.

BLUE

Rogue River Blue

Little Boy Blue

Blue cheese is defined by a blue mold added to the milk during cheesemaking. The most common type of blue mold is *Penicillium roqueforti*, made famous by Roquefort cheese. *Penicillium glaucom*, known for its use in Gorgonzola, is the other main type of mold. Both of these strains of blue molds are aerobic, meaning they require oxygen in order to bloom or develop. To allow the blue mold to grow, cheesemakers pierce the cheese with thin needle-like tools which create tunnels of air to the interior of the cheese. *Penicillium roqueforti* is most often used for blue cheeses that have a somewhat open texture: if you cut the cheese open you would see nooks and crannies (also called caves) where the curds have not knit together completely and the blue mold has grown into those spaces. *Penicillium glaucom* is used in cheeses where the curds knit together more, thus the development of the blue mold within the paste looks almost like veins rather than big blotches of blue. Common cheeses in this category are Oregon Blue, Point Reyes Original Blue, Stilton, and Two-Faced Blue.

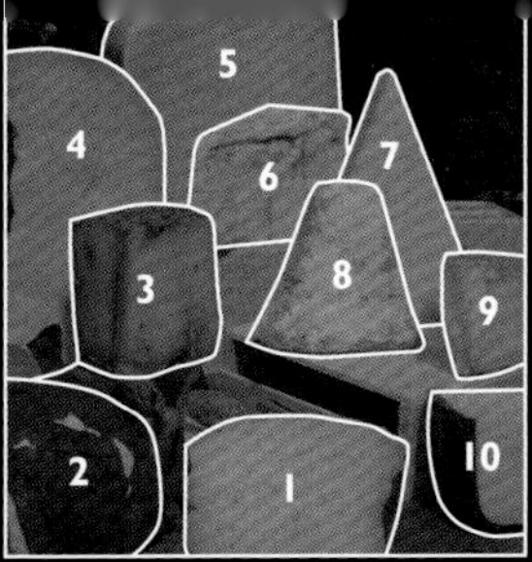

1 Black Jewels, Blue Rose Dairy
2 Up in Smoke, Rivers Edge Chèvre
3 Partly Sunny, Estrella Family Creamery
4 Tulare Cannonball, Bravo Farms
5 Asiago, Vella Cheese Company
6 Crater Lake Blue, Rogue Creamery
7 Italian Style Table Cheese, Vella Cheese Company
8 Subblime, Estrella Family Creamery
9 Caldwell Crik Chevrette, Estrella Family Creamery
10 Cayuse Mountain Goat, Larkhaven Farmstead Cheese

LEFT Freshly unhooped cheeses at Andante Dairy
BELOW LEFT A wheel of Bohemian Creamery's Capriago
BELOW Wheels of San Joaquin Gold with signature cow medallions at Fiscalini Farmstead Cheese Company
BOTTOM Weebles hanging in the cellar at Estrella Family Creamery
OPPOSITE The impressive aging room at Matos Cheese Factory

TOP Tomme from Sea Breeze Farm on Vashon Island, Washington

ABOVE A wheel of Boerenkaas at Willamette Valley Cheese Company

LEFT Sign at Marin French Cheese Company in Petaluma, California

OPPOSITE Young disks of Cirrus *(top)* and drums of Seastack developing their bloomy rinds *(bottom)* in the aging room at Mount Townsend Creamery

Cheddar production at Fiscalini Farmstead Cheese Company

LEFT TO RIGHT Step 1: Draining and raking curds

Step 2: Flipping rectangular blocks of curd

Step 3: The first of many stackings of the curd blocks

Step 4: Milling the elongated slabs of curd

Step 5: Cheesemaker Mariano Gonzalez hoists a Cheddar form freshly filled with curds.

Step 6: Wheels are coated with lard as soon as they come out of their hoops.

Step 7: Clothbound wheels age for 18–24 months in the cellar.

ABOVE Sign at the end of the road to Matos Cheese Factory

LEFT A tree-climbing Alpine goat at Rivers Edge Chèvre

BELOW An aging wheel of Guapier at Estrella Family Creamery

RIGHT Wheels of Goat Manchego aging at Bodega Artisan Cheese
BELOW A cut wheel of Two Rock Valley cheese on display at Raymond & Co. Cheesemongers
BOTTOM Drums of Mt. Tam drain after being pulled from the brine tank at Cowgirl Creamery.

A wide range of goat cheese is produced at Rivers Edge Chèvre

LEFT Chèvre draining in cloth bags

BELOW Jupiter Moon enclosed in a container for increased humidity

BOTTOM Maturing wheels of Saint Olga

OPPOSITE Stages of Sunset Bay: freshly ashed *(top)* and developing a bloomy rind *(bottom)*

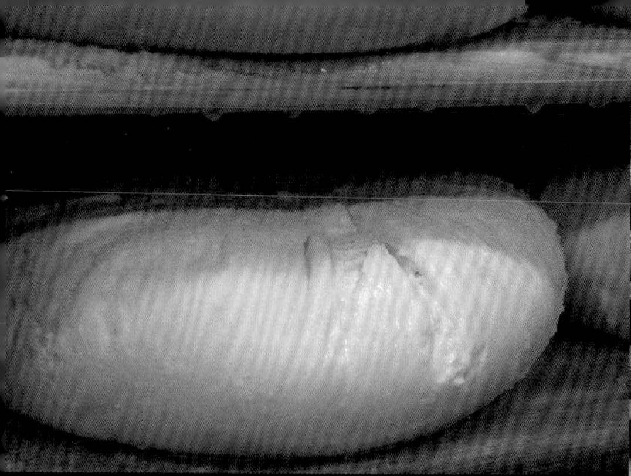

Development of Capricious at Achadinha Cheese Company
ABOVE Dry salted wheels drain on shelves in the aging room
RIGHT Wheels with mottled black, gray, and white molds creating a natural rind
BELOW Fully ripened, oil-rubbed wheel

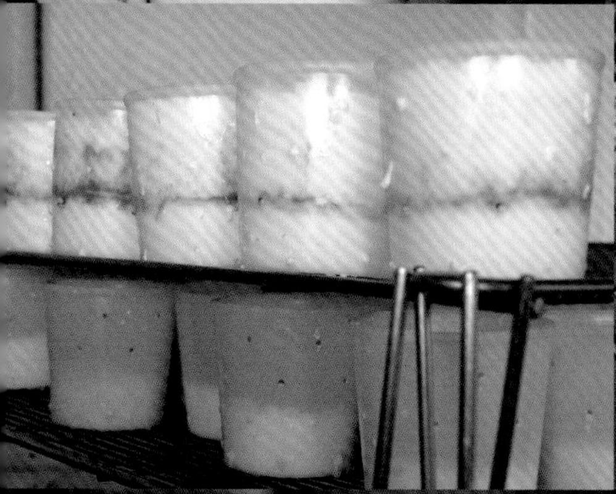

A glimpse into life at Monteillet Fromagerie

TOP LEFT Pierre-Louis Monteillet agitates milk after adding starter culture

TOP RIGHT Joan Monteillet removes drained cheeses from their forms

ABOVE LEFT Freshly made Larzacs draining in their forms

ABOVE Surface-ripened cheeses aging

LEFT Fully aged cheeses on display in the tasting room

Making Oregonzola at Rogue Creamery
TOP LEFT Scooping curds into forms
ABOVE Wheels draining via gravity
LEFT Dry salted wheels begin curing in aging rooms
BELOW Piercing wheels by machine
OPPOSITE Newly pierced wheel on a rack in the aging room *(top)* and fully developed wheel of Oregonzola cut open for tasting *(bottom)*

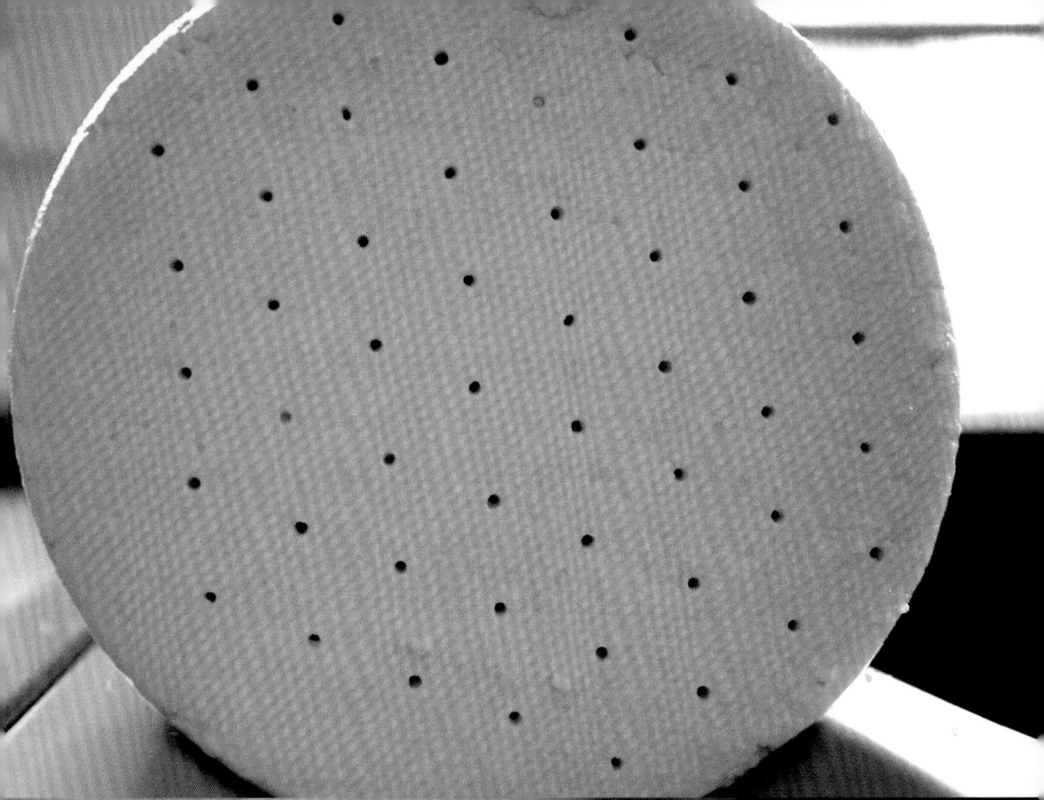

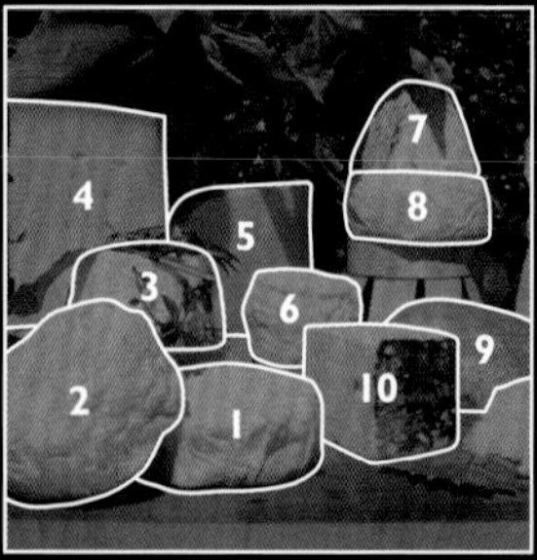

1 French Prairie, Willamette Valley Cheese Company
2 Otentique, Juniper Grove Farm
3 Spring/Summer Crottin, Rivers Edge Chèvre
4 Astraea, Rivers Edge Chèvre
5 Goat Gouda, Central Coast Creamery
6 Ripened Chevre, Port Madison Farm
7 Saint Helens, Port Madison Farm
8 Blue Moon, Port Madison Farm
9 Weebles, Estrella Family Creamery
10 UFO, Quillisascut Cheese Company

Cheese at Home

Sampling a cheese before you buy it is the easiest way to be sure of what you are getting, whether at the farmers' market, supermarket, or specialty cheese shop. If you can't taste, look carefully for signs of damage or decay.

FRESH: Tough or hardened areas on the surface. Mold of any color.

BLOOMY RIND: Dark or brown spots on the rind. Gray or dark brown color beneath the rind.

SURFACE-RIPENED: Rind looks wet or has slipped away leaving the paste exposed.

WASHED RIND: Dark brown or black marks on the rind. Dry or flakey spots on rind. Gray or brown tint to the paste.

SEMI-SOFT: Sweat beads on the cut surface. Visible cracking on the rind. Lasting aroma of ammonia.

SEMI-FIRM AND HARD: Sweat beads on the cut surface. Rind looks wet (this is fat leaching through the rind). Uneven, large cracks in the paste.

BLUE: Gray or brown tint to the paste.

CHEESE TASTING

The basics of cheese tasting are intuitive: look, smell, and taste. Unless you are planning on becoming a professional cheese taster, tasting is about waking up your senses and cataloging your likes and dislikes. Learning how to taste will help you shop for cheese more effectively.

LOOK: What color is the cheese? What type of rind does it have (bloomy, natural, waxed)? Are there any unusual cracks or holes in the paste? These observations can help you understand how the cheese was made and also identify possible defects.

SMELL: Take a good whiff of the interior of the cheese. An uneven edge releases flavors better than cut edges so, when tasting a firm cheese, it helps to break the piece in half. Don't get hung up on vocabulary, go ahead and compare the smells to things that are familiar to you. You can also crush a morsel up between your fingers and spread it out to see if more aromas are released as the cheese warms up.

TASTE: Always begin by tasting the very interior of a cheese and work your way out to the rind. The only rule about eating or not eating rind goes like this: if it tastes good to you, eat it; and if it doesn't taste good to you, don't. Work the cheese around in your mouth and be sure to wait after you swallow for the finish. Cheese can be a one-note wonder or it can have many stages of flavor—don't rush it.

As long as you pick out cheeses that taste good to you, you can't go wrong! If you are interested in a structured tasting, an easy option is to go with some kind of theme. Don't limit yourself to the ones suggested here as there are many more.

Cheese Tasting Ideas

- Get a selection of cheeses made from different milks (cow, goat, sheep, buffalo).
- Stick with one milk type and get a variety of styles (fresh, bloomy, hard).
- Select cheeses from a single country or region.
- Taste the same cheese at various ages (you'll need your cheesemonger's help with this one).
- Go vertical: select one milk type and taste in various forms from fluid milk through semi-aged and finally hard aged cheeses.

You can spruce up a cheese board with nuts or dried fruits, jams, honeys, and various breads or crackers, but serving a board devoted to cheese alone can also be a wonderful treat.

PAIRING CHEESE WITH BEVERAGES

Each cheese entry in this book includes a beverage pairing recommendation. Cheeses go beautifully with a wide range of beverages such as spirits, beer, cider, wine, and even non-alcoholic drinkable vinegars. You can either match similar flavors (bright, tangy cheese with high-acid white wine) or put opposing flavors together to balance them (bright, tangy cheese with creamy, round white wine). Generally speaking, white wines and old world reds pair well with a wide variety of cheeses, beer is an absolute workhorse when it comes to pairing with cheese plates, and fortified wines and spirits work well to highlight individual flavors in cheeses.

You can also base your pairing on a single, prominent flavor that stands out in either the cheese or the beverage. For example, with an aged mountain-style cheese, like Gruyère, you could play up a pronounced toasted nut flavor by pairing it with an oxidized sherry that shares that same note of toasted nuts. Considering texture when pairing cheese with beverages is also helpful: a decadent triple cream goes beautifully with a beverage that tempers the richness of the cheese, such as the high-acid, sparkling wine Champagne.

A good low-pressure approach to educating your palate, and having a good time, is to bring home your favorite beverages and a couple of your favorite cheeses and experiment with various combinations. Inevitably, there will be some less-than-tasty pairings, but there will also be some real winners too.

CUTTING AND SERVING

Although cutting and serving cheese is not incredibly complicated, following some guidelines will make it easier and help you get the most out of each piece.

When cutting cheese for yourself, day-to-day, the best approach is simple: lop off the bit of cheese you want to eat, then wrap up the rest and put it back in the refrigerator. Temperature changes are very hard on cheese, causing fats and flavor to sweat out and rinds to dry out and perish.

Preparing cheese for large groups calls for a different approach. You can either set out chunks of cheese on serving trays or you can cut the cheeses into individual pieces. Big chunks leave the cutting to your guests which is not the most efficient use of cheese, but slicing it all up means more of the cheeses' surface will be exposed to the air and the cheese will go downhill faster. If you go with chunks you can lay out a variety of knives on the board or platter, and maybe even a demitasse spoon for soupy washed rind cheeses. If the cheeses have been allowed to come up to room temperature guests won't need a razor sharp knife to cut them. When you slice cheeses into individual portions make sure that each serving of cheese has a bit of both the rind and the paste. For example, you should cut a Camembert or Brie like a pie rather than cutting it in a grid because you want to be sure that each piece has equal amounts gooey center and rind. Either way, for groups larger than twelve people, you can avoid congestion by making up multiple platters rather than one big board.

Helpful Tips

- Cutting soft cheese while it's still cold can help make the cuts cleaner and easier to transport to serving dishes. It's better to cut harder cheese at room temperature.
- Keep a moist cloth handy to wipe down your knife when working with sticky and clingy cheese. When cutting super crumbly blue cheese, use a warm, moist cloth as the heat will help the knife glide through the paste quickly and avoid excess crumbling.
- Prior to cutting, remove any bandaging cloth or leaves from the exterior of the cheese.
- The veins of blue mold running through the paste often make the cheese more delicate so it's best to cut blues with a sharp, thin knife or a cheese wire.
- Neat and tidy slices can get boring after a while. Learn to view crumbled and broken pieces as rustic rather than ruined.

Tools

Many cheesemakers and mongers use chef's and paring knives. Others use wires and cheese-specific tools. A well-rounded, home cheese toolkit includes a chef's knife, a knife with holes throughout the blade, a shaver, and a paring knife. When slicing cheese at home use a chef's knife for hard cheeses and get a good quality knife with holes on the blade for slicing all other styles. Shaving tools are great for hard cheeses when you want to top salads or other dishes with thin slivers. A paring knife will come in handy for petite cheeses, such as California Crottin or Inverness, which are firm but a bit small for a chef's knife.

A cheese wire is used to cut fresh, softer, and blue cheeses.

A knife with holes on the blade is ideal for cutting and serving soft to semi-firm cheese.

A cheese shaver works well for hard cheeses.

Different Cheese Shapes and How to Cut Them

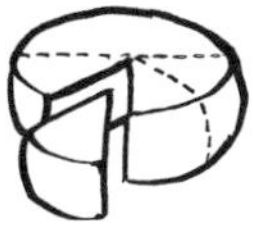

Buttons, disks, and small drums

A small, round cheese could be categorized as a button, a disk, or a small drum. Buttons range in size from one to three ounces and are often fresh or surface-ripened goat cheeses. Disks are low, flat, circular cheeses ranging from six ounces to two pounds; these are commonly surface-ripened, bloomy rind, or washed rind cheeses. Drums are cheeses whose sides are taller than their diameter.

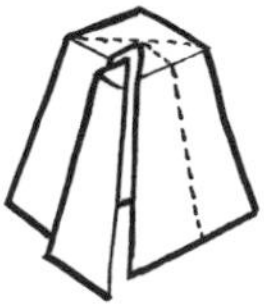

Pyramids and truncated pyramids

Pyramids and truncated pyramids range in size from five to twelve ounces. They are usually fresh, bloomy rind, or surface-ripened goat cheeses.

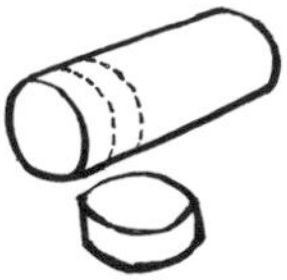

Logs

The log (or buche in French) is a common shapes for fresh, bloomy rind, or surface-ripened goat cheese. Log sizes range from three to twelve ounces.

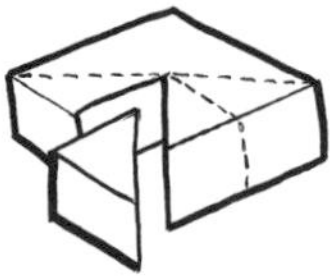

Squares

Square-shaped cheeses are not particularly common. The size ranges from eight ounces to eight pounds.

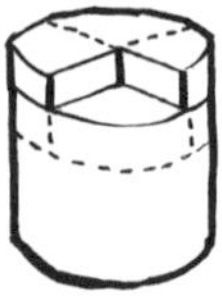

Drums

The drum is a rounded shape in which the sides of the cheese are taller than the diameter. Medium and large drums range from eight ounces to twenty pounds.

Large wheels

Small or soft wheels

The wheel is the largest category of cheese shapes because it includes all cheese types in sizes ranging from two pounds to more than one hundred pounds. It usually indicates a round cheese in which the sides are taller than a disk. Smaller wheels (up to ten pounds) or softer wheels (often blue cheese) are best cut into long, skinny triangles.

STORING

Cheese has a tendency to absorb aromas and flavors from other items in your refrigerator. It also loses moisture and flavor when exposed to air. The trick to storing cheese is to keep it in a cool enough place (38–45 degrees F) while making sure it is humid enough so that it doesn't dry out. Imagine your own skin if left exposed to a windy and brisk winter's day: that's what life in your refrigerator is like for cheese.

The best thing to do is wrap the cheese in something that will protect it from air currents while still allowing it to breathe. One option is to wrap the cheese in parchment paper, which is breathable, followed by a loose layer of plastic wrap. Many cheese retailers also sell cheese paper. This paper has two layers, one protective and one breathable, helping to keep cheese in great condition. Always store the wrapped cheese in one of the refrigerator's drawers.

If you can manage it, a smart strategy is to buy an amount of cheese that you will eat within a few days so that it never sits for very long in your fridge.

Cheese Atlas

HOW TO USE THE CHEESE ATLAS

Each cheese appears alphabetically with its producer and the producer's location, the cheese style and shape, milk type, beverage pairing suggestion, a brief description, and other information. Throughout the atlas, commonly produced cheeses and some innovative cheesemakers are also profiled.

Cheese Atlas Icons

The suggested beverage pairing for each cheese is indicated by an icon and accompanied by a specific suggestion, such as a wine varietal or style of beer.

Red wine

White wine

Sparkling wine

Dessert wine

Beer

Cider

Spirits

The type (or types) of milk used to make each cheese is indicated by an animal icon. The animal breed (or breeds) is listed next to the icon.

Cow

Goat

Sheep

Buffalo

Each cheese entry also includes:

STYLE: Fresh, bloomy rind, washed rind, surface-ripened, semi-soft, semi-firm, hard, or blue
SIZE/SHAPE: Average weight and shape (or size and shape varies)
RAW/PASTEURIZED: Indicates whether milk is raw or pasteurized
COAGULANT: Animal rennet or microbial coagulant
AFFINAGE: Minimum aging time
AVAILABILITY: Seasons listed (or availability varies)
MILK SOURCE: Farmstead or creamery
CERTIFICATIONS: If the producer has a certification it will be listed here
SIMILAR CHEESE: Lists a cheese that has similar characteristics
DESCRIPTION: Notes on the cheese, including its production, taste, and producer

Top Ten Cheeses

Asking a cheesemonger to choose her favorite cheeses is akin to asking a mother to choose her favorite child. When challenged to select my favorites, I think about those that I am most often drawn to in the cheese case when helping customers or when buying for myself. For the most part, my top ten West Coast cheeses are what I call crowd pleasers; they also show off the breadth of styles available in California, Oregon, and Washington.

Brindisi 70
Burrata 72
Caldwell Crik Chevrette 75
California Crottin 75
Cougar Gold 94
Creamy Bleu 96
El Dorado Gold 107
Inverness 131
Jupiter Moon 133
Scio Heritage 182

ACAPELLA

Andante Dairy • Petaluma, CA

Chenin blanc

Mixed herd

Surface-ripened
3 oz. disk, 4–6 oz. ashed disk, 8 oz. pyramid
Pasteurized
Microbial coagulant
Affinage of 3 weeks
Available year-round
Creamery
Similar to Valençay or Selles-sur-Cher

Soyoung Scanlan, the cheesemaker at Andante Dairy, is making this cheese in the small, whimsical shapes that are traditional for surface-ripened goat cheese. Acapella is available in a pyramid and two different sized disks, one of which has a layer of ash beneath its delicate white rind. The rinds of these cheeses, and the ash, contribute to the ripening of the paste from the outside toward the center. This makes for a slightly fluffier center and a more dense texture directly beneath the rind.

ADELLE

Ancient Heritage Dairy • Scio, OR

Oloroso sherry

Ayrshire and Guernsey

Lacaune–East Friesian cross

Bloomy rind
3–5 oz. drum
Pasteurized
Animal rennet
Affinage of 3 weeks
Available late spring through mid-fall
Farmstead
Similar to Saint-Marcellin

This small, farmstead cheese is made with a blend of sheep and cow milk. Milk from a herd of Lacaune–East Friesian crosses, a breed combination that yields a decent volume with good percentages of fats and protein, is combined with that of the Ayrshire and Guernsey cows. This mixture of milk gives the interior of Adelle a delightfully fluffy texture and the lactic tang associated with younger cow's milk cheeses. Though these small, bloomy rind cheeses are wrapped at two weeks to slow rind growth, they can be aged and eaten all the way up to five weeks.

AGED TOMME

Pug's Leap Farm • Healdsburg, CA

Old world cabernet franc

Alpine, Nubian, and Saanen

Semi-firm
3–4 lb. wheel
Raw
Animal rennet
Affinage of 2 months
Availability varies
Farmstead
Similar to Corsican Goat Tomme

This handsome, mottled gray and black tomme is dotted with splotches of white mold. The flavors are woodsy, herbaceous, and rustic, with a subtle nuttiness in the paste directly beneath the rind. When possible, this farmstead cheesemaker uses kid rennet, a coagulant that comes from the lining of a young goat's stomach and has a unique influence on flavor and texture development. Since there is not a high demand for kid rennet this coagulant is not consistently available in the United States.

ASH TOMME

Quillisascut Cheese Company • Rice, WA

Beaujolais

Primarily Alpine with crosses of Saanen and Nubian

Semi-firm
1.5 lb. wheel
Raw
Animal rennet
Affinage of 2 months
Available summer through winter
Farmstead
Similar to aged Selles-sur-Cher

These small tommes, made entirely from goat milk, are coated with ash all over the outside. Unlike many goat cheeses that are covered with ash, the Quillisascut variety is firm in texture. The ash adds an interesting grittiness and the flavors of the paste harken to the fresh and tangy French goat cheese Selles-sur-Cher. Some peppery notes fade into an overall smooth finish.

ASHED TOMETTE

Shamrock Artisan Goat Cheese • Willits, CA

IPA

Purebred Alpine, Nubian, and LaMancha

Semi-firm
6–8 oz. disk
Pasteurized
Microbial coagulant
Affinage of 2 months
Available year-round
Farmstead
Similar to aged Pélardon

Though this cheese looks like many other small-format goat cheeses, its texture makes it distinct. After draining, these small disks are not pressed. However, they are very low moisture because they are aged for a minimum of two months. A dusting of vegetable ash covers the exterior and no molds develop on the rind. The result is a dense, firm cheese with flavors of fermented fruits and a sharp peppery finish.

ASIAGO

Vella Cheese Company • Sonoma, CA

Lambrusco

Holstein and Guernsey

Semi-firm
10 lb. wheel
Raw
Microbial coagulant
Affinage of 6–12 months
Available year-round
Creamery
Similar to Asiago

This cheese is made in the likeness of the established Italian cheese Asiago. These wheels most closely resemble the younger versions of Asiago consumed either as table cheeses or used for grating. The flavor is sharp with a bit of fermented sweetness and the texture is semi-firm.

ASTRAEA

Rivers Edge Chèvre • Logsden, OR

Hefeweizen

Alpine

Semi-firm
8 lb. wheel
Raw
Animal rennet
Affinage of 4 months
Available year-round
Farmstead
Similar to Capra Valtellina

One afternoon at Rivers Edge Chèvre there was a small mishap with their famed Ilahee Tommes. The curds did not get pressed into the forms as firmly as usual and as a result the wheels came out quite tall—too tall, in fact. Because these wheels were not like all the other Ilahee Tommes, the cheesemakers decided to do something different with them during the aging process. From then on, the rinds of Astraea have been rubbed with extra virgin olive oil and spiked with a mixture of exotic spices (Vietnamese cinnamon, white pepper, and chipotle pepper) giving the wheels a lovely, deep reddish-brown color. The cheese is semi-firm in texture and has a variety of flavors ranging from dried fruits to toasted hazelnuts along with some rustic goat milk notes.

BASERRI

Barinaga Ranch • Marshall, CA

Sherry

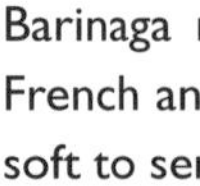

East Friesian with some Katahdin bred in for hardiness

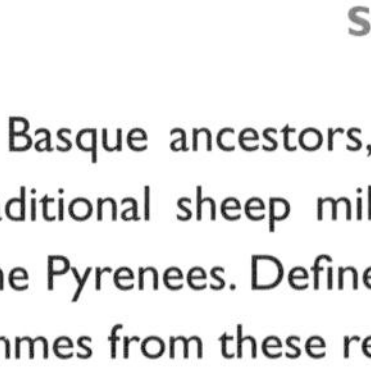

Semi-firm
4.5 lb. wheel
Raw
Animal rennet
Affinage of 2 months
Available summer through fall
Farmstead
Similar to Idiazabal and Ossau Iraty

Honoring the traditions of her Basque ancestors, owner and cheesemaker Marcia Barinaga models Baserri on traditional sheep milk cheeses made throughout the French and Spanish regions of the Pyrenees. Defined by textures ranging from semi-soft to semi-firm, sheep milk tommes from these regions are slightly sweet and nutty, and sometimes contain delicate accents of lemon. Barinaga's aged sheep milk tommes are made with milk from her East Friesian flock, which are on pasture year-round, weather permitting. She makes two tommes from the same recipe and cheesemaking process: the curds are simply scooped into two different sized forms. Baserri is the larger wheel and Emaldi is a compact two-pound tommette.

BEER CHEESE

Port Madison Farm • Bainbridge Island, WA

Stout

Nubian

Semi-firm
6.5 lb. wheel
Pasteurized
Microbial coagulant
Affinage of 2 months
Available fall through winter
Farmstead
Similar to Garrotxa

Not to be confused with the pungent Bier Kaas, a washed rind cheese made in Germany and Austria, Port Madison's Beer Cheese is a natural rind tome that is washed periodically throughout its development with a syrupy stout. The beer aids in the development of mold growth and also helps maintain moisture on the rind. The resulting cheese is mild but full-flavored with earthy notes.

BELORA

Alpine Lakes Sheep Cheese • Leavenworth, WA

Arneis

East Friesian and Lacaune with genetics from fiber sheep breeds

Bloomy rind
5–6 oz. drum
Raw
Microbial coagulant
Affinage of 2 months
Available summer through fall
Farmstead
Similar to Chaource

Belora is carefully aged over two months so that it can be made with raw milk and meet FDA regulations. The thin bloomy rind that develops has a bit of snap to it and gives way to a velvety paste. At its core, this cheese is delightfully fresh and simple almost reminiscent of a young ricotta salata. While maintaining some of the sweetness characteristic of sheep milk, this small cheese also shows vibrant fresh milk flavors common in younger cheeses.

BERMUDA TRIANGLE

Cypress Grove Chevre • Arcata, CA

Barbera

Mixed herd

Surface-ripened
1 lb. elongated triangle
Pasteurized
Microbial coagulant
Affinage of 3 weeks
Available year-round
Creamery
Similar to aged Valençay

Leave it to Cypress Grove Chevre's founder, Mary Keehn, to create another iconic surface-ripened goat cheese. This long, low triangle, a radical shape for cheese, was designed to offer chefs an interesting alternative for cheese plates, which are often filled with wedges cut from round cheeses. The shape's impact on the texture is huge: a large surface area means a large population of bacteria working hard to quickly break down the paste. The very center of the triangle is fluffy and tangy while the surrounding paste is smoother and can become more piquant. The triangles are sprinkled with ash when they come out of their forms and encouraged to develop a thin, white rind.

BLACK BUTTE

Pedrozo Dairy and Cheese Company • Orland, CA

Gewürztraminer

Holstein and Jersey

Semi-firm
20 lb. wheel
Raw
Microbial coagulant
Affinage of 6 months
Available mid-fall through winter
Farmstead
Similar to Abondance

The Pedrozos learned to make one style of cheese from their predecessors at the farmstead dairy that they now own and operate. Black Butte is essentially the reserve version of that cheese, Northern Gold, with some important modifications. Black Butte is made only during the spring when pastures are at their peak and the milk is loaded with natural flora that work well for longer aging. Curds are packed into large molds that will yield wheels that weigh twenty pounds or more. Once the wheels come out of their forms they are brined before going into the aging room. Throughout the six-month aging period, wheels are repeatedly rubbed down to discourage the development of molds. The paste is craggy in texture and loaded with flavors of butter and tropical fruit like pineapple.

BLACK CREEK BUTTERY

Estrella Family Creamery • Montesano, WA

Brown or red ale

Primarily Normandy

Semi-firm
12 lb. wheel
Raw
Animal rennet
Affinage of 6 months
Available year-round
Farmstead
Similar to Cheddar crossed with Emmental

These handsome drums are made in two versions, one unadulterated and the other studded with chunks of jalapeño. Though this cheese does not have Cheddar in its name, it does follow the procedures for traditional Cheddar: cooking, cheddaring, milling, and pressing. The ferment-flavored paste has a firm texture that becomes smooth on the palate rather than breaking up into granular pieces. Both the interior and the rind are hues of deep gold.

BLACK JEWELS

Blue Rose Dairy • Winlock, WA

Assyrtiko

Primarily Saanen and Alpine

Semi-soft
4–5 lb. wheel
Raw
Animal rennet
Affinage of 10 weeks
Available year-round
Farmstead
Similar to lightly salted feta

The rind of this large, springy tomme is rubbed with charcoal giving it a dramatic appearance. The paste has an open texture, pocked in many small openings, and is creamy on the tongue with a bit of a roux-like consistency. The cheese has a pleasant acidity, alongside more vegetal flavors reminiscent of lettuce or wet grass.

BLACK SHEEP TOMME

Black Sheep Creamery • Adna, WA

Tawny port

East Friesian and Rideau Arcott

Semi-firm
3.5–4.25 lb. wheel
Raw
Microbial coagulant
Affinage of 5–7 months
Available in fall
Farmstead
Similar to aged pecorino

The procedure for making this tomme is similar to that used for producing the other aged sheep cheeses at Black Sheep Creamery, but since different cultures are used the resulting cheese is quite different as well. The firm paste of Black Sheep Tomme tastes of brown butter and toast.

Although Black Sheep Creamery has their own flock of sheep and produces mainly farmstead cheeses, they also make Tin Willow Tomme, a non-farmstead, pasteurized version of Black Sheep Tomme with milk they purchase from a sheep dairy in Oregon. The recipe and cultures are exactly the same but because the milk comes from sheep that inhabit a different landscape, the flavors that develop in the cheese are unique. The sheep at Tin Willow farm eat sagebrush and alfalfa hay and so an herbaceous, slightly woody flavor comes through in the paste alongside the toasted notes.

BLONDIE'S BEST

Pedrozo Dairy and Cheese Company • Orland, CA

Barbera

Holstein and Jersey

Semi-firm
2 lb. wheel
Raw
Microbial coagulant
Affinage of 2 months
Available year-round
Farmstead
Similar to Ubriaco

These compact tommes are made with milk from the Pedrozo farm's Holstein and Jersey cow herd. This breed combination supplies a good yield, boosts the components for cheesemaking, and gives the paste its rich yellow color. Blondie's Best is bendy and slightly dry in texture. The paste has an aroma of fermented grapes and flavors of rendered butter and hay.

Pedrozo makes several variations of this cheese: Tipsy Cow is soaked in red wine, Stout Cow is soaked in Sierra Nevada stout, and Bubbly Cow is soaked in a California sparkling wine. All varieties are made from raw milk and aged for a minimum of sixty days.

BLUE MOON

Port Madison Farm • Bainbridge Island, WA

Cava

Nubian

Surface-ripened
8–9 oz. drum
Pasteurized
Microbial coagulant
Affinage of 2 weeks
Available spring through fall
Farmstead
Similar to Chaource

Cheesemaker Steve Phillips uses a mold that is no longer commercially available to develop the delicate bloom on his surface-ripened cheeses. This mold was the standard for Camembert until 1905, when researchers in France found a mold strain that was more predictable, *Penicillium Camemberti*, and persuaded producers to switch. The older strain has gone off the market entirely in the United States but Phillips has maintained the culture at his cheese facility because he finds it works well with his cheeses. Blue Moon has a slight snap to the rind, a nice delicate breakdown beneath, and a firm but moist cakey center. The paste has flavors of artichoke and a hint of brown butter. Occasionally the exterior molds will take on a bluish cast as the drums age, hence the name Blue Moon.

BOERENKAAS

Willamette Valley Cheese Company • Salem, OR

Prosecco

Jersey

Semi-firm
12 lb. wheel
Raw
Microbial coagulant
Affinage of 4 months
Available year-round
Farmstead
Similar to traditional Gouda

This raw milk tomme is only made when the cows can be out on pasture, which, in Oregon's Willamette Valley, is about six to seven months of the year. Wheels are aged a minimum of four months and some stock is reserved and aged longer so that the cheese can be available year-round. The pure milkiness of the paste is a great example of the complexity of flavor inherent in milk, as notes range from acidic fresh-curd to rich hints of caramel. The producer also makes a pasteurized version of this cheese year-round called Farmstead Gouda.

BOHO BEL

Bohemian Creamery • Bodega, CA

Sauterne

Jersey

Surface-ripened
3 lb. wheel
Pasteurized
Microbial coagulant
Affinage of 6–8 weeks
Available year-round
Creamery
Similar to Bel Paese

Modeled on the classic Italian cheese Bel Paese, this semi-soft wheel made from organic Jersey milk is beefy in flavor. The texture of the paste at the interior part of the wheel is like moist clay, while the bit directly bordering the rind is more sturdy and dense. The rind looks rough and crumbly but actually adds a nice toothsome texture and contrast to the thick paste.

BO POISSE

Bohemian Creamery • Bodega, CA

Marc de Bourgogne

Jersey

Washed rind
.75 lb. square
Pasteurized
Microbial coagulant
Affinage of 6–8 weeks
Available winter through early spring
Creamery
Similar to Pavé d'Auge

Loosely based on the recipe for the famed stinky French cheese Epoisses, this cheese resembles another French cheese called Pavé d'Auge because of its shape. The squares of Bo Poisse are washed with a brine solution throughout their development. The resulting orange-brown rinds are pocked with tufts of white bloom and are quite tacky to the touch. The use of high fat content organic milk from Jersey cows gives the paste a texture similar to butter. Even with a heft of pungent, washed rind flavor you can still taste the sweetness of the milk. This cheese is only made during the fall and winter months when conditions in northern California are ideal for its aging.

BOVONCINO

Bohemian Creamery • Bodega, CA

Dry cider

Jersey

Semi-firm
2 lb. wheel
Pasteurized
Microbial coagulant
Affinage of 6–8 weeks
Available year-round
Creamery
Similar to Salva Cremasco

This is basically a cow milk version of the creamery's original goat cheese called Capriago. Co-owner Lisa Gottreich lived and worked in Italy for years and has crafted her cheeses in hopes of recreating some of her Italian favorites. Bovoncino is also made in a larger, four-pound wheel called Boviago. Both wheels have a rich, golden-colored paste because of the Jersey milk used to make them, and a rugged natural rind. The paste has a lively sour cream flavor and hints of onion; closer to the rind it gets a bit dusty and earthy.

BREWLEGGIO

Estrella Family Creamery • Montesano, WA

Pike Brewing Ale

Fino sherry

Primarily Normandy

Washed rind
3 lb. wheel
Raw
Animal rennet
Affinage of 2 months
Available year-round
Farmstead
Similar to Taleggio

Modeled on a traditional Italian washed rind cheese called Taleggio, wheels of Brewleggio are washed during their aging with ale donated by local Pike Brewery. The ale provides much needed moisture and food for the *Brevibacterium linens* that help wheels develop their flavorful, rust-colored surface. The paste tastes of butter and brine and the rind has notes of bittersweet chocolate. Though not quite as pudgy as Italian Taleggio, Brewleggio has a soft, tacky texture that melts on the tongue rather than sticking.

10 BRINDISI

Willamette Valley Cheese Company • Salem, OR

American sparkling

Jersey

Hard
9–10 lb. wheel
Raw
Microbial coagulant
Affinage of 8 months
Available year-round
Farmstead
Similar to aged fontina

Brindisi is the maiden name of cheesemaker and owner Rod Volbeda's mother. The recipe for this cheese is based on the well-known Italian cheese fontina. Though most of the Italian fontina found in the United States is young and quite soft, there are also mature fontinas that are aged longer and often classified as a hard, grating cheese. This cheese, made in Oregon's Willamette Valley, has a natural rind and a fudgy, firm paste riddled with crystals. Underlying flavors of brown butter and roasted hazelnuts are heightened by hints of lemon and a balanced dose of salt.

BRONCHA

Achadinha Cheese Company • Petaluma, CA

Riesling

Mixed herd

Semi-firm
5 lb. wheel
Pasteurized
Microbial coagulant
Affinage of 3 months
Available year-round
Farmstead
Similar to Corsican goat tomme

Broncha is reminiscent of some of the finest European farmhouse goat tommes because of its rustic, craggy exterior that is speckled with gray and white molds. The firm yet crumbly paste smells sweet, like cooked milk. That sweetness comes through on the palate but is balanced by salty notes. Also detectable are subtle earthy flavors common in aged goat's milk cheeses. If you are particularly lucky, you might even find a spot of wild blue mold that has bloomed in the paste, a welcome addition Broncha's flavors. This cheese tastes wonderful with a dollop of dark cherry preserves.

BUCHE

Juniper Grove Farm • Redmond, OR

Oregon pinot noir

Mixed herd

Surface-ripened
6.5 oz. log
Raw
Microbial coagulant
Affinage of 2 months
Available year-round
Farmstead
Similar to Sainte-Maure Caprifeuille

This classic, surface-ripened log has a sprig of straw running through its center. Made from raw goat milk, these logs must age for two full months to be in accordance with the raw milk guidelines in the United States. Rustic flavors of hay and barnyard emerge on the rind and the center shows off the natural acidity of young goat cheese.

BUCHE

Pug's Leap Farm • Healdsburg, CA

Cabernet franc

Mixed herd

Surface-ripened
5–7 oz. log
Pasteurized
Animal rennet
Affinage of 2–3 weeks
Available late spring through early winter
Farmstead
Similar to Pierre Dorée

This log-shaped goat cheese grows a slightly downy white rind as it ages. Throughout its development, Buche loses moisture and eventually the paste is firm enough that it breaks into shards when cut. The paste has a somewhat sharp, fermented fruit flavor.

BUCHERET

Redwood Hill Farm • Sebastopol, CA

Chablis

Alpine, LaMancha, Nubian, and Saanen

Bloomy rind
5 oz. drum
Pasteurized
Microbial coagulant
Affinage of 3 weeks
Available year-round
Creamery
Kosher and Certified Humane Raised and Handled
Similar to chevrot

This compact, goat milk, bloomy rind cheese is made with lactic coagulation. While a small dose of coagulant is added to the milk, the curd formation mainly happens through natural acidification of the milk over a long enough period of time. This is akin to what happens to abandoned milk in your refrigerator—solids will naturally form and clump together—but it is controlled during the making of Bucheret so the flavors of the curd don't become overly acidic. The paste has a lemony flavor at its center, surrounded by a ring that is dense in texture, all wrapped in a snappy rind.

10 BURRATA

Gioia Cheese Company • South El Monte, CA

Lambrusco

Holstein

Fresh
1 lb. ball
Pasteurized
Microbial coagulant
No affinage
Available year-round
Creamery
Similar to Italian burrata

Burrata is basically a purse of stretched mozzarella curd that is filled with a mixture of un-stretched curd mixed with cream and a dash of cultures. Today a lot of mozzarella is stretched by machines which allows producers to churn out higher volumes for a lower cost. Burrata is generally made by hand because of its juicy filling and the gentle handling required to stretch the curd around the filling, and as a result it is more tender and luscious than mozzarella. The filling of curds and cream is cultured to give the cheese a slightly sour flavor that combines nicely with the sweet, milkiness of mozzarella. Burrata is often served with a bit of olive oil and salt.

CABECOU

Laura Chenel's Chevre • Sonoma, CA

Cabernet franc

Mixed herd

Fresh
2 oz. button
Pasteurized
Microbial coagulant
Affinage of 7–10 days
Available year-round
Creamery
Similar to fresh crottin

Cabecou are small buttons of fresh goat cheese that are popped out of their forms after draining and dried for a few days in the haloir or drying room. After they are sufficiently dry, they are placed in olive oil with rosemary, thyme, and bay leaf. The texture of the paste is fudgy, like clay, and has a cool and smooth feeling on the palate. Grassy notes and the herbs provide savory depth to the young, tangy cheese.

CABRALINDA

Nicolau Farms • Modesto, CA

Rioja

Primarily Alpine

Semi-firm
5 lb. wheel
Raw
Microbial coagulant
Affinage of 3 months
Available mid-spring through mid-fall
Farmstead
Similar to Manchego crossed with Cheddar

Cabralinda is meant to resemble Manchego although traditionally it would be made with sheep milk. These goat milk wheels firm up as they age, the paste maintaining a smooth texture even though it is marked with some small holes. The flavors of a Manchego exist in the sweet, sweaty notes though some sharpness comes through as the wheels mature.

CABRERO

Bodega Goat Cheese • Lakeport, CA

Ruby port

French Alpine, Saanen, and LaMancha

Semi-firm
3 lb. wheel
Raw
Microbial coagulant
Affinage of 6 months
Available fall through winter
Farmstead
Similar to Manchego

Cabrero is a Manchego-style aged goat cheese with a twist. These medium-sized wheels are aged soaking in wine made by the cheesemakers. The varietal of the wine changes from year to year— past grapes include petit syrah and merlot. The paste has a goaty herbaceous flavor combined with vibrant fruit notes from the wine.

CAERPHILLY

Gothberg Farms • Bow, WA

Blond ale

LaMancha

Semi-soft
4–6 lb. wheel
Pasteurized
Animal rennet
Affinage of 6 months
Available fall through spring
Farmstead
Similar to young Cheddar

Caerphilly is a traditional Welsh cow milk cheese that is moist and crumbly at its innermost point and more dense and creamy toward the rind with flavors of buttermilk and mushrooms. Rhonda Gothberg has made this recipe her own by using goat milk instead of cow milk. Wheels are air-dried for one week and then coated with a breathable, thin wax for the duration of their affinage. Aged to six months, the semi-soft wheels retain a nice amount of moisture and the bright, tangy paste definitely honors the flavors of traditional Caerphilly.

10 CALDWELL CRIK CHEVRETTE Estrella Family Creamery • Montesano, WA

Oloroso sherry

Primarily Normandy

Primarily LaMancha

Washed rind
1 lb. wheel
Raw
Animal rennet
Affinage of 2 months
Available spring through fall
Farmstead
Similar to Muenster

Caldwell Crik is the name of the creek that runs through the Estrella Family's farm and Chevrette is the French term which describes cheese made from a combination of cow and goat milk. This washed rind cheese achieves robust, complex flavors without going overboard on pungency. The wheels are actually low disks made in a basket mold that leaves a pattern on the toothsome but edible rind. The paste is smooth and creamy in texture and filled with notes of toasted almonds and hazelnuts that compliment the beefy flavor.

10 CALIFORNIA CROTTIN Redwood Hill Farm • Sebastopol, CA

Vouvray

Alpine, LaMancha, Nubian, and Saanen

Surface-ripened
3 oz. button
Pasteurized
Microbial coagulant
Affinage of 2 weeks
Available year-round
Creamery
Kosher and Certified Humane Raised and Handled
Similar to crottin

This cheese is modeled on a classic French goat cheese, Crottin de Chavignol, from the Loire Valley region. The crinkly, thin skin, the main characteristic of a crottin, results from the addition of *Geotrichum*, a mold added to the milk along with other cultures. Immediately beneath that skin is a dense, almost creamy layer that takes on flavors of hay and brioche at about three weeks and becomes increasingly peppery as the cheese ages. The heart of California Crottin remains lighter in color and in the early stages has a cakey texture and tangy flavor, becoming more meaty and robust with time. California Crottin is a beautiful accompaniment to salads and works well as an after-dinner cheese served with a bit of floral honey, like clover or lavender.

CAMELLIA

Redwood Hill Farm • Sebastopol, CA

Prosecco

Alpine, LaMancha, Nubian, and Saanen

Bloomy rind
5 oz. disk
Pasteurized
Microbial coagulant
Affinage of 3–4 weeks
Available year-round
Creamery
Kosher and Certified Humane Raised and Handled
Similar to Camembert crossed with Saint-Félicien

The silky texture of Camellia's paste is the result of its large curds, which retain more moisture than curds that have been cut down small. The creamery uses milk from their herd of goats at Redwood Hill Farm, the first Certified Humane goat dairy in the United States, to produce this Camembert-style cheese.

CAPRAPHILLY

Dee Creek Farm • Woodland, WA

Belgian white

Nubian and Nigerian Dwarf

Semi-firm
10 lb. wheel
Raw
Microbial coagulant
Affinage of 3 months
Available year-round
Farmstead
Similar to young pecorino

These wheels are a beautiful bone-white color. When cut, the network of connected curds is still visible in the paste, a telltale sign that the texture of this cheese is more springy than creamy. The flavors are mild but retain the lively, sweetness of fresh goat milk.

CAPRIAGO

Bohemian Creamery • Bodega, CA

Nero d'Avola

Primarily Alpine

Semi-firm
4 lb. wheel
Pasteurized
Microbial coagulant
Affinage of 6–8 weeks
Available year-round
Creamery
Similar to young Asiago

This goat milk tomme is made to resemble Italian Asiago, which is traditionally made with cow milk. The wheels are bathed in brine early on during their development. Fully aged wheels have a faint aroma of dusty blue cheese, possibly from the combination of molds that develop on the rind. The paste, both moist and crumbly, has hints of toasted pine nuts and almonds.

CAPRICIOUS

Achadinha Cheese Company • Petaluma, CA

Macvin du Jura

Mixed herd

Hard
9 lb. square
Pasteurized
Microbial coagulant
Affinage of 3 months
Available year-round
Farmstead
Similar to Mahón

The shape of this cheese is created by wrapping a mound of curd in a square section of cheesecloth, winding the ends of the cloth together, and then knotting and tucking the cloth on the underside of the curds. Boards are stacked between layers of the newly formed wheels, creating a gentle pressing, and the cheeses are left to drain. The resulting squarish cheese displays sinewy lines on the exterior and an indentation from the knot. Aromas of toasted nuts arise when cutting into the dark brown- and rust-colored tomme. The texture is slightly grainy without feeling sandy on the tongue. The paste has some tangy flavors, not quite as lemony as those found in chèvre, that make this aged goat cheese so refreshing.

CAPRINO ROMANO

Gothberg Farms • Bow, WA

Tocai

LaMancha

Semi-firm
4–6 lb. wheel
Pasteurized
Animal rennet
Affinage of 9 months
Available winter through summer
Farmstead
Similar to Capra Valtellina

Caprino Romano is a nod to the great family of Romano cheese from Italy. These wheels are made with milk from twenty LaMancha goats that browse on the Gothberg Farms acreage. In addition to natural forage, the goats are fed high-quality alfalfa hay from eastern Washington, pea hay from the local Skagit Valley, and a custom grain mix from a local mill. The effort that goes into caring for the goat herd is manifest in the clean, fresh flavor of the paste, which becomes increasingly complex the longer the wheels are aged.

CAPRONCINO

Bohemian Creamery • Bodega, CA

Orkney Scotch (Scapa)

Primarily Alpine

Semi-firm
2 lb. wheel
Pasteurized
Microbial coagulant
Affinage of 6–8 weeks
Available year-round
Creamery
Similar to Capra Valtellina

The rinds of these wheels have a light gray hue and are marked on the top and bottom by the basket molds in which they are formed. After coming out of their forms, the wheels are washed for the first two weeks and then sprayed with a *Penicilium candidum* mold. The wheels are flipped but get no further washing for the remaining four to six weeks of the aging process. The paste has a wide range of flavors including hints of wild onion and sweet toffee, followed by a woodsy finish.

CARDABELLA

Monteillet Fromagerie • Dayton, WA

Old world sauvignon blanc

Alpine

East Friesian–Lacaune cross

Surface-ripened
3 oz. button
Pasteurized
Microbial coagulant
Affinage of 2 weeks
Available spring through fall
Farmstead
Similar to Saint-Marcellin

Cardabella changes with the shifts in milk production at the Monteillet's farm. When the sheep are in milk these small disks are composed entirely from sheep milk, as their supply dwindles goat milk is added into the mix. Both versions are simple and elegant with earthy flavors and limited salt. The paste has a velvety texture and the thin skin that develops on the surface is supple and imparts a mellow hay flavor.

Sustainability Spotlight: Monteillet Fromagerie

After working for a decade as conventional wheat farmers, Joan and Pierre-Louis Monteillet decided to become small, farmstead dairy operators. In 2001, when wine production was really taking off, they saw an opportunity for cheesemaking in the Walla Walla region of Washington. A native Frenchman, Pierre-Louis knew how fantastic cheese was supposed to taste. That knowledge, combined with incredible gumption, led them to build the Fromagerie.

Understanding that their farm was located in a growing tourist region, the Monteillets have always looked for ways to diversify and increase revenue streams to the farm. In doing this, some financial pressure was removed from their start-up cheese operation. In addition to growing their herds of goats and sheep, they fixed up an old building on their property and transformed it into a lovely home that is now rented out by farm visitors or those passing through wine country.

The Fromagerie was built with a tasting room that stocks wines from the region alongside the Monteillet's goat and sheep milk cheeses, allowing it to fit seamlessly into the wine trail. Joan also offers cheesemaking workshops and has created an internship program for those interested in learning more about all aspects of the farm. The Monteillets have worked hard to meld with their surrounding agricultural community and to create a small, sustainable ecosystem on their thirty-one acres complete with the dairy and cheesemaking, free-range poultry, whey-fed pigs, and an organic garden.

CARMELA

Goat's Leap • Saint Helena, CA

Chablis

LaMancha

Semi-firm
5 lb. wheel
Raw
Animal rennet
Affinage of 4 months
Available late winter through spring
Farmstead
Similar to Ibores

Carmela is a tidy five-pound tomme, bone-white at its innermost point and becoming slightly beige toward the rind. Although the producers at Goat's Leap milk fewer than fifteen goats, they make seven different kinds of cheese. This means that all of their products are perennially in short supply, Carmela included, so each is a treasure to be cherished. Carmela's dusty gray exterior and pockmarked paste is suggestive of some of the firm, Spanish goat milk tommes. The cheesemaker is willing to release some wheels at four months but will often hold them back until they are six to eight months old to allow for even more flavor development.

CARMODY

Bellwether Farms • Petaluma, CA

New world chardonnay

Jersey

Semi-firm
3.5 lb. wheel
Pasteurized
Microbial coagulant
Affinage of 6 weeks
Available year-round
Creamery
Similar to young pecorino

Inspired by the rustic Italian cow milk cheese called Toma, the cheesemaker at Bellwether developed this rich and buttery tomme. They sell two versions: Carmody is often dipped in wax and aged out to six weeks, and Carmody Reserve is unwaxed and aged for a minimum of three months. At both ages, the paste is creamy on the palate. In the Reserve wheels, buttery flavors take on a cultured edge similar to a slightly soured cream and the texture becomes a bit more dense and fudgy. All wheels are aged on pine planks because pine does not transfer any flavors or aromas to the cheese.

CASCADIA

Fairview Farm • Dallas, OR

Old world pinot noir

Alpine, Nubian, and Alpine–Nubian cross

Semi-soft
4 lb. wheel
Raw
Microbial coagulant
Affinage of 2 months
Available summer through winter
Farmstead
Animal Welfare Approved
Similar to Ticklemore

This farmstead tomme is one of three cheeses made from the same basic recipe at Fairview Farm. Cascadia is a spaceship-shaped wheel with a mottled gray rind and an organized pattern of indentations from its basket form. The milk comes from a farmstead herd of sixteen goats that are allowed to browse when weather permits. The curds are washed before being drained and the wheels are lightly pressed and brined. This vibrant cheese has a backbone of woodsy flavors and sweeter, cooked milk notes on the finish.

CASCADIAN FRECHETTE

Goldin Artisan Goat Cheese • Molalla, OR

Muscadet

Mostly Alpine

Washed rind
.5–1 lb. drum
Pasteurized
Animal rennet
Affinage of 5–6 weeks
Available late spring through early winter
Farmstead
Similar to Garrotxa

Although these wheels are washed periodically throughout the aging process, they do not develop the tacky, rust-colored exterior typical of washed rind cheeses. Instead the washing works to keep the rinds healthy and supple and limit mold development to a minimum. The portly drums do not develop a great deal of pungency instead they lean toward milder, herbaceous goat milk flavors.

CAUSSE NOIR

Monteillet Fromagerie • Dayton, WA

Old world pinot gris

Alpine

East Friesian and Lacaune

Semi-firm
6 lb. wheel
Raw
Animal rennet
Affinage of 3 months
Available late summer through fall
Farmstead
Similar to Lavort

Causse Noir is a mixture of two-thirds goat milk and one-third sheep milk from Monteillet's own herds. These semi-firm tommes develop a natural rugged and crusty rind but are rubbed with salt to inhibit the growth of molds. The sheep milk adds a nuttiness, like that found in tommes produced in the French and Spanish Pyrenees, and the goat milk keeps the texture on the lighter side even though it melds into a smooth paste on the tongue. Because of the high demand, wheels are often released after three months; when wheels are allowed to age longer they develop crunchy tyrosine crystals throughout the paste.

CAVEMAN BLUE

Rogue Creamery • Central Point, OR

Tojkai

Brown Swiss, Holstein, and Brown Swiss–Holstein cross

Blue
5 lb. wheel
Raw
Microbial coagulant
Affinage of 1 year
Available year-round
Creamery
Similar to Cashel Blue

Caveman Blue is a modification of a natural rind blue recipe that Rogue tinkered with for more than five years. The recipe is designed to create wheels that can be aged for long periods of time without losing their creamy texture. Allowing the cheese to develop a natural rind, rather than dipping it in wax or aging it in plastic, has a huge impact on the texture and even the flavors that evolve. The veins have an assertive blue mold flavor and the melt-on-the-tongue texture is similar to butter. The minimum affinage is one year but some batches, depending on flavor development, are held up to six months longer.

CAYUSE MOUNTAIN GOAT — Larkhaven Farmstead Cheese • Tonasket, WA

Aged Maury

Mixed herd

Semi-soft
4.5–5 lb. wheel
Raw
Animal rennet
Affinage of 5–7 months
Available year-round
Farmstead
Similar to young Gouda

Larkhaven is a farmstead producer milking twenty-five goats in the central part of northern Washington. Their goats are on pasture, weather permitting, and are dried off for a couple months in the winter. Cayuse Mountain Goat is available year-round because it is aged out for a minimum of five months and the producers carefully manage their inventory to stretch through the dry season. The wheels are dipped in wax so the cheese maintains a moist, fudgy consistency. The paste has a tangy flavor and an underlying sweetness of cooked milk.

CECILIA — Estrella Family Creamery • Montesano, WA

Vin Santo

Primarily LaMancha

Semi-firm
5 lb. wheel
Raw
Animal rennet
Affinage of 4 months
Available spring through fall
Farmstead
Similar to Capra Valtellina

Cheesemaker Kelli Estrella drew her inspiration for Cecilia from an Italian aged goat milk cheese that won huge accolades at the World Cheese Awards. A tall wheel with a dry, firm texture, the paste has deep, savory flavors of chestnuts and earthy herbs. The cheese is well-salted without tasting salty.

CERTOUX

Goldin Artisan Goat Cheese • Molalla, OR

Muscadet

Mostly Alpine

Semi-firm
1.75–2 lb. wheel
Pasteurized
Animal rennet
Affinage of 5–6 weeks
Available late spring through early winter
Farmstead
Similar to young Ticklemore crossed with Gubbeen

This washed goat milk tomme has a basket-weave-imprinted rind that is bright orange with spots of brown and white. The paste is light and cakey at the interior and has flavors of pine nuts and Meyer lemon. Directly beneath the rind the paste becomes thicker and a bit creamy.

CHAPARRAL

Rinconada Dairy • Santa Margarita, CA

White Burgundy

Nubian

East Friesian–Lacaune cross

Semi-firm
1 lb. wheel
Raw
Animal rennet
Affinage of 2 months
Available late spring through early fall
Farmstead
Similar to Ibores

Chaparral is a tidy tomme made from raw goat and sheep milk. This cheese has a dusty blond rind and enough moisture in the semi-firm paste to make it smooth on the tongue. Flavors of brown butter and toast are followed by a sharp finish. This cheese tastes lovely grated over a salad or savory dish, or accompanied by a rich chestnut honey.

CHAROLAIS

Bodega Artisan Creamery • Bodega, CA

Old world chenin blanc

Alpine

Surface-ripened
8–10 oz. column
Raw
Microbial coagulant
Affinage of 2 months
Available summer through early winter
Farmstead
Similar to French Charolais

These goat cheese columns, with soft, pudgy-looking, wrinkled rinds, appear identical to their French namesake. Curds are placed in tall forms that look like tumblers and flipped frequently for the first twenty-four hours to ensure a proper barrel-shape. Flavors range from slightly funky and earthy near the rind to crisp and acidic at the center of this small cheese.

CHEDDAR

Red ale (mild Cheddar), IPA (sharp Cheddar)

Cheddar is a name that can be given to any cheese made in any style, as it is not a protected cheese name like Parmigiano-Reggiano. As a result of not being protected, the name Cheddar is a bit diluted and can mean many things. Cheese that can be described as traditional Cheddar (or having been made in the traditional method) must go through the cheddaring and milling processes. Keep in mind that many, if not most, cheeses called Cheddar have *not* been cheddared and milled.

The cheddaring step takes place after cutting the curds and draining the whey. The curds are allowed to mat together along the bottom of the vat after they are raked to either side, divided approximately in half. These so-called walls of curd are cut into equal-sized rectangular slabs. Cut slabs are stacked and flipped at specific intervals to continue to mat the curds together, stretch it slightly, and press out additional moisture. There is a steady, controlled increase in acidity as lactic bacteria metabolize lactose into lactic acid. This acidity impacts the texture of the curds and ensures the durability of the cheese over longer aging times.

Once curds have been cheddared they are milled. This means that each slab is fed through a mill that cuts them up into finger-sized rectangles. Milling releases a bit more moisture and sets the curds up to be evenly salted.

An alternative to the traditional method is called stirred-curd which involves cutting the curds, gradually heating them to a specific temperature, and then stirring constantly for a set period of time. The stirring and heating are both intended to encourage the curds to release moisture. Once the stirring ends, the curds are drained, poured into forms, and pressed before being packaged for aging. Cheddars are produced in two basic shapes: blocks and wheels.

BLOCK CHEDDARS

Block Cheddars are semi-soft and semi-firm cheeses whose curds have been scooped into large, rectangular block forms, pressed, and sealed in cryovac plastic for aging. Depending on the cultures used, the aging of block Cheddars can range from two weeks to ten years. The resulting cheeses are usually forty-pound blocks that get cut down into the small rectangles, loaves, and squares that are found on supermarket and cheese shop shelves. A natural coloring called annatto is sometimes added to block Cheddars to produce an orange hue. Block Cheddars are produced in a variety of styles such as medium, sharp, and extra sharp. These terms are not universal so sharp Cheddar can vary significantly from one producer to another.

Many of the block Cheddar producers listed here are making multiple varieties including mild, medium, sharp, extra sharp, and flavored. Block Cheddars can be made with raw or pasteurized milk and either type of coagulant (animal or microbial).

 **Appel Farms**

 **Bravo Farms**

 **Fiscalini Farmstead Cheese Company**

 **Loleta Cheese Factory**

 **Meyenberg Goat Milk Products**

 **Redwood Hill Farm**

Rogue Creamery

Rumiano Cheese Company

Sierra Nevada Cheese Company

Spring Hill Cheese Company

Tillamook County Creamery

Vella Cheese Company

Washington State University Creamery

Willamette Valley Cheese Company

CHEDDAR WHEELS

Most Cheddar wheels fall into the semi-firm category. Some wheel-shaped Cheddars are sealed in a thick plastic or coated with wax, like the blocks, but others are bandaged with cheesecloth (clothbound) or left to develop a basic, natural rind. Each method of aging, combined with the cheese's production, yields different results.

Bravo Farms
SILVER MOUNTAIN AGED CLOTHBOUND CHEDDAR
Raw • Clothbound • Microbial coagulant • Affinage of 1 year • Creamery

Estrella Family Creamery
BLACK CREEK BUTTERY
Raw • Clothbound • Animal rennet • Affinage of 6 months • Farmstead

Fiscalini Farmstead Cheese Company
EXTRA MATURE BANDAGE WRAPPED CHEDDAR
Raw • Clothbound • Microbial coagulant • Affinage of 18 months • Farmstead

VINTAGE BANDAGE WRAPPED CHEDDAR
Raw • Clothbound • Microbial coagulant • Affinage of 2 years • Farmstead

Golden Glen Creamery

CHEDDAR IN THE RAW

Raw • Natural rind • Microbial coagulant • Affinage of 6 months • Farmstead

MEDIUM CHEDDAR

Raw • Natural rind • Microbial coagulant • Affinage of 3 months • Farmstead

RIVER CHEDDAR

Raw • Natural rind • Microbial coagulant • Affinage of 1 year • Farmstead

Gothberg Farms

CHEDDAR

Raw • Sealed rind • Animal rennet • Affinage of 1 year • Farmstead

Port Madison Farm

FARMHOUSE CHEDDAR

Pasteurized • Clothbound • Microbial coagulant • Affinage of 6 months • Farmstead

Samish Bay Cheese Company

MONT BLANCHARD

Pasteurized • Sealed rind • Microbial coagulant • Affinage of 2 months • Farmstead

Silver Springs Creamery

JEDDAR

Raw • Sealed rind • Animal rennet • Affinage of 6 months • Farmstead

Steamboat Island Goat Farm

AGED RAW CHEDDAR

Raw • Sealed rind • Microbial coagulant • Affinage of 2 months • Farmstead

Vella Cheese Company

DAISY RAW MILK CHEDDAR

Raw • Sealed rind • Microbial coagulant • Affinage of 1 year • Creamery

CHE VIN

Dee Creek Farm • Woodland, WA

Red ale

Nubian and Nigerian Dwarf

Semi-soft
4 lb. wheel
Raw
Microbial coagulant
Affinage of 2 months
Available year-round
Farmstead
Similar to Murcia al Vino (Drunken Goat)

The recipe for Che Vin is a modified Gouda made from raw goat milk. The wheels are pressed and then soaked for a minimum of sixty days, though sometimes up to four months, in a variety of local wines (like blackberry or pinot noir), hard cider, or whatever alcoholic beverage local producers are making. The rind color is ever-changing, but the paste always has a smooth, closed texture and is subtly infused with flavors of the soaking liquid.

CHEVITO

Yerba Santa Goat Dairy • Lakeport, CA

Muscadet

French Alpine, Saanen, and LaMancha

Semi-firm
1 lb. wheel
Raw
Microbial coagulant
Affinage of 3 months
Available mid-summer through winter
Farmstead
Similar to French feta

Chevito wheels are allowed to develop a natural, moldless rind so their exterior is an off-white color. The cheesemaker compares the paste to that of an unbrined French feta because it is pocked with holes, retains quite a bit of moisture throughout its aging, and is not salty like other styles of feta.

CHÈVRE

Sancerre

Chèvre is the French word for goat and is also the name for fresh goat milk cheese. In the United States, all chèvre is made with pasteurized goat milk because federal and state regulations dictate that any cheeses aged less than sixty days must be made from pasteurized milk.

Post-pasteurization, the milk must be cooled slightly so that starter cultures will be able to survive and get down to the business of metabolizing lactose (the naturally occurring sugar in milk) into lactic acid. This process continues without disturbance for up to twenty-four hours until the acid levels rise enough to encourage delicate curds to form. Often a very small amount of coagulant is added to aid in the formation of curds.

The curds are placed into various-shaped forms or mesh bags and allowed to drain for another twenty-four hours. The resulting cheese is versatile, pillowy, and often tangy; a perfect canvas for adding herbs and spices or for dropping into a salad or quiche. Chèvre that will be marinated is often allowed an extra day or two for drying which will help the pieces absorb the seasoned oils surrounding them.

Andante Dairy
Plain, flavored, and marinated • Creamery

Blue Rose Dairy
Plain and flavored • Farmstead

Cypress Grove Chevre
Plain and flavored • Creamery

Dee Creek Farm
Plain and flavored • Farmstead

Ferns' Edge Goat Dairy
Plain and flavored • Farmstead

Fraga Farm
Plain, flavored, and marinated • Farmstead

Gothberg Farms
Plain • Farmstead

Grace Harbor Farms
Plain and flavored • Farmstead

Harley Farms
Plain, flavored, and marinated • Farmstead

Juniper Grove Farm
Plain and flavored • Farmstead

Laura Chenel's Chevre
Plain and flavored • Creamery

Monteillet Fromagerie
Plain, flavored, and marinated • Farmstead

Mystery Bay Farm
Plain and flavored • Farmstead

New Moon Goat Dairy
Plain and flavored • Farmstead

Nicolau Farms
Plain • Farmstead

North Valley Farms Chevre
Plain and Flavored • Farmstead

Port Madison Farm
Plain and flavored • Farmstead

Quail Croft Farmstead Cheese
Plain and flavored • Farmstead

Redwood Hill Farm
Plain • Creamery

Rivers Edge Chèvre
Plain, flavored, and marinated • Farmstead

River Valley Cheese
Plain and flavored • Farmstead

Shamrock Artisan Goat Cheese
Plain and flavored • Farmstead

Sierra Nevada Cheese Company
Plain • Creamery

Silver Falls Creamery
Plain and flavored • Farmstead

Siskiyou Crest Goat Dairy
Plain • Farmstead

Yerba Santa Goat Dairy
Plain and flavored • Farmstead

CHUBUT

La Mariposa • Sweet Home, OR

Verdicchio

Holstein

Semi-soft
1.25 lb. or 3.5–4 lb. wheel
Pasteurized
Microbial coagulant
Affinage of 4–5 weeks
Available year-round
Creamery
Similar to Toma

La Mariposa's cheesemaker, Mariano Battro, has recreated a cheese from his native country of Argentina. Chubut is a traditional Argentinean cheese made from a recipe developed by Welsh settlers in the late 1800s. These small, natural-rinded wheels have a smooth, closed paste, pure flavors of butter, and a hint of dusty cellar.

CINCO ESQUINAS

La Mariposa • Sweet Home, OR

Sauvignon blanc

Holstein

Semi-firm
14 lb. wheel
Raw
Microbial coagulant
Affinage of 3 months
Available year-round
Creamery
Similar to provolone

Cheesemaker Mariano Battro keeps the rinds free of gray, brown, green, and blue molds by repeatedly wiping down the cheeses during aging, resulting in wheels with a clean yet slightly rough exterior. Though Cinco Esquinas tastes similar to provolone, it was modeled after Swiss-style mountain cheeses and this influence is apparent in the pliable texture of the paste. Flavors of sweet butter are followed by a sharp, nearly acrid finish.

CIRRUS

Mount Townsend Creamery • Port Townsend, WA

Sweet riesling

Holstein

Bloomy rind
5 oz. disk
Pasteurized
Microbial coagulant
Affinage of 1 month
Available year-round
Creamery
Similar to Camembert

A Pacific Northwestern take on Camembert, Cirrus has a delicate bloomy rind and a silky paste. The lower fat content in the Holstein milk, which Mount Townsend Creamery buys from a local farmer, gives these disks a lighter texture than the tacky and blobby paste of a traditional French Camembert. The dominant flavor is freshly salted butter with an occasional small bite on the finish.

CLABBERED COTTAGE CHEESE

Cowgirl Creamery • Petaluma, CA

Chenin blanc

Holstein, Jersey, and Holstein–Jersey cross

Fresh
8 oz. tub
Pasteurized
Microbial coagulant
No affinage
Available year-round
Creamery
Certified Organic

The process for making this unique cottage cheese begins with nonfat, organic milk that is transformed into curds, each just slightly smaller than an eraser on a pencil. The curds are then drained, combined with cream that has been cultured, and allowed to rest until they thicken and develop a tangy flavor. The combination of the sturdy but pliable small curds and clabbered cream makes a luscious, lactic, and flavorful cottage cheese. A perfect way to enjoy this cheese is with fresh, summer tomatoes, a dash of sea salt, and a crack of fresh pepper.

CLASSIC

Silver Springs Creamery • Lynden, WA

Belgian ale

LaMancha and Alpine

Semi-firm
10 lb. wheel
Pasteurized
Animal rennet
Affinage of 7–8 months
Available year-round
Creamery
Similar to goat Gouda

These bone-white wheels are made with goat milk from the cheesemaker's herd of LaManchas and supplemental milk from a neighboring dairy farm. The wheels are aged long enough to develop a craggy, semi-firm texture. The flavors are similar to those found in Gouda-style cheeses aged much longer than seven to eight months. Both the sweetness of caramelized milk and the savory flavors of earth and salt are apparent at once. Although Classic is made seasonally, in line with the goats' lactation cycle, it is available almost year-round because the longer aging period gives the producer an opportunity to stagger its release.

CLASSICO

Tumalo Farms • Bend, OR

Trappist ale

Saanen and French Alpine

Semi-firm
9–10 lb. wheel
Raw and Pasteurized available
Animal rennet
Affinage of 4 months
Available year-round
Farmstead
Similar to goat Gouda

During the production of Classico, the curds are washed (to control the acidity and keep the curds flexible) and cooked (to extract moisture). These steps, combined with the fresh goat milk from Tumalo Farms, yields a paste that is semi-firm but still springy. The sweetness is balanced by a fermented, tangy note that becomes more pronounced as the cheese ages. The recipe used to make Classico is also used to create some flavored varieties: Capricorns with rainbow peppercorns, Fenacho with fenugreek, and Antigo with cumin.

10 COUGAR GOLD

Washington State University Creamery • Pullman, WA

Sauvignon Blanc

Holstein

Semi-firm
30 oz. disk
Pasteurized
Microbial coagulant
Affinage of 1 year
Available year-round
Creamery
Similar to Cheddar crossed with Gouda

Cougar Gold's long and illustrious history began in the 1930s when the recipe was created at Washington State University's Creamery. Plastic packaging had not yet been invented so the University staff devised a method for packaging the cheese in cans. Milk for the creamery has always been provided by the University's cow dairy. The culture for this unique cheese was obtained in the 1940s and has been maintained and continually used ever since. The cheese does not use a traditional Cheddar culture but the curds are cheddared in the cheesemaking process. The curds are pressed overnight and then cut into disks that fit in the thirty-ounce cans. The paste is like a dry clay, flaking apart in large, thin shards and becoming creamy and dense on the tongue. Sweet flavors of caramel are balanced by a hint of bittersweet chocolate and tangy, sharp notes on the finish.

COVERED BRIDGE

Pholia Farm • Rogue River, OR

Moscato d'Asti

Nigerian Dwarf

Semi-soft
3.5 lb. domed wheel
Raw
Microbial coagulant
Affinage of 4 months
Available late spring through early summer
Farmstead
Similar to Castelrosso

This wheel stands out because of its shape which is like an egg with a slightly flattened top and bottom. The natural rind is a rugged, dusty, gray-brown, and the texture is fatty and luscious without being creamy. The paste smells sweet, likely a result of washing the curds and from adding Wild River Brewery's Nut Brown Ale during the cheesemaking process. The flavor is woodsy and contains hints of sour cream and notes of blue mold. While the goats are bred year-round to keep a steady supply of milk, Covered Bridge is made in small quantities in the spring and only available to retail outlets within the region.

CRATER LAKE BLUE

Rogue Creamery • Central Point, OR

Pinot blanc

Brown Swiss, Holstein, and Brown Swiss–Holstein cross

Blue
5 lb. wheel
Raw
Microbial coagulant
Affinage of 4 months
Available year-round
Creamery
Food Alliance Sustainable Producer
Similar to Bleu d'Auvergne

This is the first blue cheese designed by Cary Bryant and David Gremmels since taking ownership of Rogue Creamery in 2002. Their goal was to create a contemporary blue cheese that encompassed the great complexity of flavor associated with old world blues. They achieved this by using a combination of blue mold strains that yield both brilliant, sharp notes and earthy flavors. The paste melts like butter on the tongue.

CREAM CHEESE

Cream cheese is basically a fresh cheese made with pasteurized cream and whole milk. The old-fashioned method of making cream cheese involves a coagulant and time: the cream and milk are allowed at least twelve hours to gently set before the curds are washed. This process helps the curds retain some sweetness and a more flexible texture, without adding the stabilizers or gums that are frequently used in more mass-produced cream cheese.

Bodega Artisan Cheese
Plain and flavored • Microbial coagulant • Farmstead

Jacobs Creamery
Plain and flavored • Microbial coagulant • Creamery

Meyenberg Goat Milk Products
Plain and flavored • Microbial coagulant • Creamery

Sierra Nevada Cheese Company
Plain • Microbial coagulant • Creamery

10 CREAMY BLEU

Alpine Lakes Sheep Cheese • Leavenworth, WA

Old world pinot noir

East Friesian and Lacaune with genetics from fiber sheep breeds

Blue
5–6 oz. drum
Raw
Microbial coagulant
Affinage of 2 months
Available summer through fall
Farmstead
Similar to Hubbardston Blue

Roqueforti blue molds added to the milk during cheesemaking give this cheese a broad bouquet of flavors. The interior has funky, hay-like undertones balanced by bright, lactic notes. Directly beneath the thin, gray-blue rind is a slightly creamy paste which has modest hints of smoke. Creamy Bleu is mainly sold near the small farm where it is produced, in the foothills of the Cascade Range east of Seattle.

CREAMY CHEESE

Silver Springs Creamery • Lynden, WA

Txakolina

LaMancha and Alpine

Semi-soft
10 lb. wheel
Pasteurized
Animal rennet
Affinage of 2 months
Available year-round
Creamery
Similar to Garrotxa

This farmstead cheesemaker is still growing so the milk produced by his herd of LaMancha and Alpine goats (fed largely on browse and pasture) is supplemented with that of a neighboring goat dairy. The wheels of Creamy Cheese have the appearance of a young goat Gouda because their uniform rinds are covered with a protective, breathable coat, and the color of the paste is bright white. The flavors range from fresh and herbaceous to toasted and slightly sweet. The texture breaks down into a smooth paste on the tongue. Minimum aging for these wheels is two months but they can be aged for six to eight months and maintain a balance of flavors and smooth texture.

CRÈME FRAÎCHE

Crème fraîche production begins with high-fat cream, double the fat content used to make sour cream (approximately 40 percent versus 18 percent). The cream is warmed to create an ideal growth environment for the added cultures. The cultures convert lactose (the naturally occurring sugars in milk) into lactic acid, creating the distinct tangy flavor in the finished product. This fermentation also thickens the cream a bit.

Because crème fraîche has a higher fat content than sour cream it is more versatile in cooking. The higher fat content not only caries more flavor but also makes crème fraîche less prone to liquefying when added to hot dishes. Crème fraîche also lacks the various fillers and stabilizers that are often added to sour cream to give it more body.

Bellwether Farms
Farmstead

Cowgirl Creamery
Creamery

El Michoacano
Creamery

Kendall Farms
Creamery

CRESCENZA

Bellwether Farms • Petaluma, CA

Sangiovese

Jersey

Semi-soft
3 lb. square or 7 oz. packet
Pasteurized
Microbial coagulant
Affinage of 2–3 weeks
Available year-round
Creamery
Similar to Stracchino

Crescenza is a classic, soft, northern Italian cheese often used in risotto or dolloped atop pizza. The walnut-sized curds are bigger than curds cut for a firm, aged cheese because larger curds retain more moisture and give Crescenza its silky and unctuous texture. This cheese is tacky to the touch but melts as soon as it hits your tongue. Crescenza from Bellwether Farms is even more luscious than some Italian versions because the producer uses milk from a neighbor's herd of Jersey cows, which are known for their high fat content milk. Although the cheese is allowed to mature for a couple weeks and develop a yeasty flavor, it retains a freshness that balances out the heft of fermentation.

CROFTER'S SWARD

Quail Croft Farmstead Cheese • Friday Harbor, WA

Old world pinot noir

Primarily Saanen

Semi-firm
6 lb. or 8 lb. wheel
Raw
Animal rennet
Affinage of 2 months
Available late spring through early winter
Farmstead
Similar to Chevrotin des Bauges

The name Crofter's Sward comes from an Old English term for lush green covering, a nod to the pastures and browse available to the goats. All of the milk from the twelve goats at Quail Croft is transformed into cheese. The wheels are made from washed curds and allowed to develop a velvety, mottled gray, brown, and black rind like rustic European tommes. The paste is smooth and has flavors of earth and nuts.

CROTTIN

Vouvray

A number of West Coast producers are making some version of this button-shaped, iconic French goat cheese. Crottin can be eaten fresh or aged out to five or six weeks and used as a grating cheese. Fresh crottin are tangy and slightly more dense than chèvre. Aged crottin are allowed to drain and for the surface to dry just enough so that the yeasts and molds added to the milk can develop a rind. Some West Coast crottin are encouraged to develop a delicate bloom and others have a wrinkly, surface-ripened skin. The length of affinage and rind development impact the texture and flavors: when young, the paste can mimic the flavors of a slightly less vibrant chèvre, with age, it can become nutty and even peppery. Chèvre chaud, a circular slice of crottin broiled atop a piece of toast, is a delicious way to enjoy this cheese.

Andante Dairy

CROTTIN

Surface-ripened • 2 oz. button • Pasteurized • Microbial coagulant • Affinage of 23–25 days • Available year-round • Creamery

Juniper Grove Farm

THOR'S SPECIAL CROTTIN

Fresh (smoked) • 5 oz. button • Pasteurized • Microbial coagulant • Affinage of 4–5 days • Available year-round • Farmstead

Laura Chenel's Chevre

CABECOU

Fresh (marinated) • 2 oz. button • Pasteurized • Microbial coagulant • Affinage of 5–7 days • Available year-round • Creamery

CROTTIN

Bloomy rind • 3 oz. button • Pasteurized • Microbial coagulant • Affinage of 12–14 days • Available year-round • Creamery

Mystery Bay Farm

CROTTIN

Surface-ripened • 4 oz. button • Pasteurized • Microbial coagulant • Affinage of 10–14 days • Available spring through fall • Farmstead

Pine Stump Farms

CROTTIN

Fresh or surface-ripened • 4–5 oz. button • Pasteurized • Microbial coagulant • Affinage of 0–14 days • Available spring through fall • Farmstead

Port Madison Farm

RIPENED CHEVRE

Surface-ripened • 4 oz. button • Pasteurized • Microbial coagulant • Affinage of 3 weeks • Available spring through fall • Farmstead

Redwood Hill Farm

CALIFORNIA CROTTIN

Surface-ripened • 3 oz. button • Pasteurized • Microbial coagulant • Affinage of 2 weeks • Available year-round • Creamery

Rivers Edge Chèvre

SPRING/SUMMER CROTTIN

Fresh • 3 oz. button • Pasteurized • Animal rennet • Affinage of 4–5 days • Available year-round • Farmstead

CROTTIN

Mystery Bay Farm • Nordland, WA

Muscadet

American Alpine

Surface-ripened
4 oz. button
Pasteurized
Microbial coagulant
Affinage of 10–14 days
Available spring through fall
Farmstead
Similar to crottin

The Crottin of Mystery Bay Farm is essentially a delicately ripened chèvre. Fresh curds are ladled into button-shaped forms and left alone until they knit together enough to maintain their shape. Once they come out of the forms they are allowed to develop a thin skin. The bacteria and yeasts that make up this skin work on breaking down the paste. The paste loses a bit of moisture and becomes more dense than fresh chèvre.

CURADO

Quillisascut Cheese Company • Rice, WA

Albariño

Primarily Alpine with crosses of Saanen and Nubian

Semi-firm
2.5–3 lb. wheel
Raw
Animal rennet
Affinage of 2 months
Available summer through winter
Farmstead
Similar to Ibores

Curado, a staple at the Quillisascut farmstead, is designed to be aged for at least two months but can be carried out over four months. At that point, the wheels are sold under the name Viejo and are suitable for grating. Young wheels are also firm in texture and lack any mold growth on the rind. The paste has winey fruit flavors and a subtle sweetness that becomes milder as the wheels age. Quillisascut Cheese Company also produces versions of Curado that have been smoked or enhanced with herbs and spices.

CURDS

Most cheese curds are based on Cheddar recipes but some producers sell curds from mozzarella or jack production too. To make sturdy, finger-sized, snackable cheese curds, producers go through the initial steps of cheesemaking—ripening, culturing, coagulating, cutting, stirring, and even salting—but stop short of scooping the curds into forms to drain or pressing them into shapes to age.

It's best to eat curds soon after they are made because they have lost moisture during the cutting, stirring, and salting stages and can become dry if aged for long periods of time. Cheese curds available in the United States are always made with pasteurized milk. In addition to plain curds, many producers add herbs and other seasonings to make a variety of flavored curds.

Appel Farms
Plain and flavored • Microbial coagulant • Farmstead

Beecher's Handmade Cheese
Plain and flavored • Microbial coagulant • Creamery

Golden Glen Creamery
Plain • Microbial coagulant • Farmstead

Rogue Creamery
Plain and flavored • Microbial coagulant • Creamery

Rumiano Cheese Company
Plain • Microbial coagulant • Creamery

Samish Bay Cheese Company
Plain • Microbial coagulant • Farmstead

Spring Hill Cheese Company
Plain and flavored • Microbial coagulant • Creamery

CYLAS

Dee Creek Farm • Woodland, WA

Red ale

Nubian and Nigerian Dwarf

Semi-firm
4 lb. wheel
Raw
Microbial coagulant
Affinage of 2 months
Available year-round
Farmstead
Similar to Colby

This raw milk cheese is made to resemble Colby, a mild-flavored cheese which is often compared to Cheddar even though it doesn't go through the cheddaring process. The curds of Cylas are washed before being scooped into forms to drain and this contributes to the mild, gentle flavors in the paste and the creamy texture on the palate. A subtle sweet flavor comes through from the goat milk.

DAFNE

Goat's Leap • Saint Helena, CA

Verdicchio

LaMancha

Surface-ripened
14 oz. disk
Pasteurized
Animal rennet
Affinage of 2 weeks
Available year-round
Farmstead
Similar to Chaource

Dafne is the Greek term for bay leaf as well as the name of these spritely goat milk disks. Each piece is enrobed in a slightly puffy, white rind and adorned with a single bay leaf. The paste is cakey, and manages to be tangy without crossing over to sharp flavors. The bright notes enhance the underlying mild, fresh goat milk flavor.

DELICE DE LA VALLEE

Delice de la Vallee • Sonoma, CA

Prosecco

Mixed herd

Mixed herd

Fresh
7 oz. tub
Pasteurized
Microbial coagulant
No affinage
Available year-round
Creamery
Kosher
Similar to fromage frais

Sheana Davis developed this mixed milk cheese because she saw an unfulfilled need among chefs for a workable, flavorful, fresh product in the kitchen. Delice de la Vallee is a combination of whole cow milk, cow milk cream, and goat milk. The texture is rich and the consistency is similar to roux. A zesty lemon note stands out in the flavors of cream and fresh milk.

DOMINOES

Estrella Family Creamery • Montesano, WA

 *Jura*

 *Primarily Normandy*

Semi-firm
.75 lb. wheel
Raw
Animal rennet
Affinage of 2 months
Available year-round
Farmstead
Similar to Tomme de Savoie

These compact wheels are formed by hand-pressing lightly cooked curds into small forms. The surface develops a speckled, grayish-white rind during the two-month affinage. Because the wheels are quite small they lose enough moisture during their aging to become semi-firm; if allowed to age longer they turn into a nice grating cheese. The flavors are a combination of fresh milk, brine, and a hint of tang. In the spring, cheesemaker Kelli Estrella also makes a leaf-wrapped version of this cheese using leaves from her neighbor's chestnut and maple trees. The adorned wheels are called Leaf-Wrapped Dominoes.

DRY JACK

 *Ale*

Created by Vella Cheese Company, Dry Jack is an American original. Dry Jack is essentially traditional jack cheese that has had more moisture expelled during cheesemaking and has been aged out longer to intensify and transform the brown butter flavors into rich toffee notes. Dry Jack has great appeal with consumers because it can be eaten as is or used as a grating cheese.

The squarish wheels are formed by wrapping the curds in cheesecloth, pulling the four corners of the cloth together, and twisting and tucking them beneath the newly formed wheel. The freshly bound cheeses are stacked in rows with boards between each layer. This weight presses the cloth knots into the underside of each wheel and leaves an indentation. Vella Cheese Company also decided to rub the outside of the wheels with oil and powdered cocoa to discourage mold growth and other producers have followed suit.

Rumiano Cheese Company

DRY MONTEREY JACK

Hard • 8 lb. square • Pasteurized • Microbial coagulant • Affinage of 9 months • Available year-round • Creamery

Spring Hill Cheese Company

ORGANIC DRY JACK

Semi-firm • 8 lb. square • Pasteurized • Microbial coagulant • Affinage of 9 months • Available year-round • Creamery • Certified Organic

Vella Cheese Company

VELLA DRY JACK

Hard • 8 lb. square • Pasteurized • Microbial coagulant • Affinage of 7 months • Available year-round • Creamery

DUTCHMAN'S FLAT

Juniper Grove Farm • Redmond, OR

Marsanne

Mixed herd

Surface-ripened
2 lb. wheel
Raw
Microbial coagulant
Affinage of 2–3 months
Available year-round
Farmstead
Similar to Selles-sur-Cher

The geographic namesake for this cheese (Dutchman's Flat is a large, often snow-covered, open plain, just below Oregon's Mount Bachelor) is echoed in the uncommon shape and size of these wheels. The low, large, flat disks measure eight inches wide by two inches high. The shape allows for a large surface area that is covered with an active, wrinkly rind working to break down the paste. The flavors progress from sharp and yeasty to a milky finish. The toothsome rind is a nice companion to the softer paste.

ECHO MOUNTAIN

Rogue Creamery • Central Point, OR

Ruby port

Brown Swiss, Holstein, and Brown Swiss-Holstein cross

Mixed herd

Blue
5 lb. wheel
Raw
Microbial coagulant
Affinage of 8–24 months
Available mid-fall through early summer
Creamery
Similar to Bleu d'Auvergne

The only mixed milk cheese offered by Rogue Creamery, wheels of Echo Mountain are highly coveted. This cheese is produced seasonally because the dairy providing the goat milk does not milk their animals year-round. Each batch has 80 percent cow milk, from a Food Alliance Certified producer, and 20 percent goat milk. Though the goat milk makes up only a portion of the raw materials it does lighten the texture and impart a bit of acidity to the paste. The blue mold used in this recipe is an earthy strain that ultimately produces a mild, approachable blue flavor.

ECLIPSE

Goat's Leap • Saint Helena, CA

Blauer Zweigelt

LaMancha

Surface-ripened
.75 lb. or 1.25 lb. wheel
Pasteurized
Animal rennet
Affinage of 7–10 days (small wheel); 2 weeks (larger wheel)
Available year-round
Farmstead
Similar to Humboldt Fog

Eclipse is a barrel-shaped, white-rinded cheese made entirely with milk from Goat's Leap's herd of LaManchas. The wheels have a streak of ash cutting through the center and a dusting of ash below their rind. The paste beneath the rind is transformed into a creamier texture while the center remains fluffy. Each wheel is crowned with star anise.

10 EL DORADO GOLD

La Clarine Farm • Somerset, CA

IPA

Alpine

Semi-firm
3.5–4 lb. wheel
Raw
Animal rennet
Affinage of 2 months
Available summer through mid-winter
Farmstead
Similar to Raclette

These wheels are named for the gold rush history of the Sierra Nevada foothills, the region in which El Dorado Gold is produced. The rind has some dark, golden colors as a result of being alternately washed and brushed throughout its aging. Solidly in the semi-firm category the texture is pliable but not sticky. The flavors are meaty yet slightly sweet and have a subtle milky tang on the finish. This cheese is full-flavored without being overwhelmingly strong.

ELK MOUNTAIN

Pholia Farm • Rogue River, OR

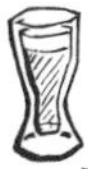

Brown ale

Nigerian Dwarf

Semi-firm
6–8 lb. wheel
Raw
Microbial coagulant
Affinage of 6 months
Available summer through winter
Farmstead
Similar to Castelmagno

The dark brown rind of this tomme is imprinted with the pattern of its basket-style form. Cheesemaker Gianaclis Caldwell bathes the wheels in a local ale from Wild River Brewery. Carrying the relationship with the brewery even further, Gianaclis also feeds her goats spent brewers grain because it is loaded with beneficial nutrients. The paste is firm and a bit crumbly.

EMERALD CITY BLUE

Port Madison Farm • Bainbridge Island, WA

Tawny port

Nubian

Blue
12–15 lb. wheel
Pasteurized
Microbial coagulant
Affinage of 4–6 months
Available late fall through winter
Farmstead
Similar to Stilton

In celebration of late fall, Port Madison Farm rolls out wheels of goat milk blue that resemble traditional English Stilton. These large wheels develop craggy natural rinds, a nice contrast to the smooth, bone-white paste streaked with blue mold.

ESTERO GOLD

Valley Ford Cheese • Valley Ford, CA

Valpolicella

Jersey

Semi-firm
6 lb. or 10 lb. wheel
Raw
Animal rennet
Affinage of 6 months
Available year-round
Farmstead
Similar to Montasio

The third generation dairy farming family that runs this farmstead operation decided to expand into cheesemaking in 2008 and Estero Gold is their inaugural cheese. The wheels are made in the style of a classic Italian cheese called Montasio known for its full flavor and dense paste riddled with small holes. This cheese is made in two different sizes, both of which have moist but firm pastes, bold, fermented fruit flavors, and a touch of sharpness on the finish.

EWE-NIQUE

Central Coast Creamery • Oakdale, CA

Pale ale

Holstein

Mixed herd

Semi-soft
9 lb. wheel
Pasteurized
Microbial coagulant
Affinage of 6 months
Available year-round
Creamery
Similar to young Gouda

Blending sheep and cow milk not only increases the potential volume of cheese but also creates a creamier texture in the paste. Although these wheels are firm enough to withstand cutting, the paste still holds quite a bit of moisture. The sheep milk offers fattier flavors of nuts and cooked milk while the cow milk carries acidity and lactic notes that keep the overall flavor balanced.

FARMER'S CHEESE

Juniper Grove Farm • Redmond, OR

Dolcetto

Mixed herd

Semi-soft
4 lb. wheel
Raw
Microbial coagulant
Affinage of 2 months
Available year-round
Farmstead
Similar to loaf mozzarella

Farmer's cheese is the term often used to describe simple, fresh cow milk cheese but the cheesemaker at Juniper Grove has created a unique, aged version. The paste is pliable and slices easily. Fresh and simple flavors have a hint of sweetness and not much salt.

FARM HOUSE

Fraga Farm • Sweet Home, OR

Fresh
3 lb. wheel
Pasteurized
Microbial coagulant
Affinage of 4–5 days
Available year-round
Farmstead
Certified Organic
Similar to queso blanco

Lager

Alpine, Nubian, and Alpine–Nubian cross

This is an interesting cheese reminiscent of queso blanco, which is normally made with cow milk, but with the rustic, earthy flavors more common to goat milk. The tall wheels are not allowed to form any rind and are sold a few days after they are made. Though the cheese crumbles a bit when cut, the texture is creamy. Flavored versions of Farm House are also available.

FARMHOUSE CHEDDAR

Port Madison Farm • Bainbridge Island, WA

Semi-firm
6 lb. wheel
Pasteurized
Microbial coagulant
Affinage of 6 months
Available spring and summer
Farmstead
Similar to Chevre Noir

Sherry

Nubian

Farmhouse Cheddar wheels have a smooth, off-white rind, likely a result of brine soaking and some rubbing throughout its aging to prevent the growth of molds. The paste has flavors of raw almonds and hazelnuts. These sweet and refreshing flavors are balanced by salt, giving this cheese an overall savory tone.

FARMSTEAD GOUDA

Pleasant Valley Dairy • Ferndale, WA

Lighter syrah

Mixed herd

Semi-soft
2 lb. or 6 lb. wheel
Raw
Animal rennet
Affinage of 2 months
Available year-round
Farmstead
Similar to young Gouda

The recipe for these wheels, dipped in bright red wax, was originally developed by Pleasant Valley cheesemakers when they started their creamery in the early 1970s. The milk comes from their mixed herd of cows that are out on pasture whenever weather permits. The paste is creamy in texture and contains a grassiness that is reminiscent of Cheddar, beefy notes, and a hint of dulce de leche.

FETA

Feta was traditionally made only from sheep milk, though today it is made from combinations of all three major milk types: cow, sheep, and goat. In the European Union the name *Feta* is protected by the government and must be produced according to approved specifications, but no such guidelines exist in the United States. Feta's production is similar to that of other semi-firm cheeses: the milk is warmed and ripened with culture, coagulant is added, curds develop, and curds are cut and scooped into forms.

Once the curds have drained, at least partially, they are salted and then stored and aged in bins filled with brine or a mixture of whey (reserved from the cheesemaking) and brine. Because the cheese is kept in this saline liquid it does not form a rind.

Feta is often salty to taste and crumbly in texture but it should also maintain lactic, sweet flavors from the milk and a creamy feel on the tongue. It is a flavorful addition to salads, savory pastries, and even quiche.

Achadinha Cheese Company
Pasteurized • Microbial coagulant • Farmstead

Alsea Acre Goat Cheese
Pasteurized • Microbial coagulant • Farmstead

Ancient Heritage Dairy
Pasteurized • Microbial coagulant • Farmstead

Appel Farms
Pasteurized • Microbial coagulant • Farmstead

Belfiore Cheese Company
Pasteurized • Microbial coagulant • Creamery

Blue Rose Dairy
Pasteurized • Animal rennet • Farmstead

Bodega Artisan Cheese
Raw • Microbial coagulant • Farmstead

Dee Creek Farm
Raw • Microbial coagulant • Farmstead

Fraga Farm
Raw • Microbial coagulant • Farmstead

Golden Glen Creamery
Pasteurized • Microbial coagulant • Farmstead

Gothberg Farms
Raw • Animal rennet • Farmstead

Harley Farms
Pasteurized • Microbial coagulant • Farmstead

Juniper Grove Farm
Raw • Microbial coagulant • Farmstead

Larkhaven Farmstead Cheese
Raw • Animal rennet • Farmstead

North Valley Farms Chevre
Pasteurized • Microbial coagulant • Farmstead

Redwood Hill Farm
Raw • Microbial coagulant • Creamery

River Valley Cheese
Pasteurized • Microbial coagulant • Farmstead

Samish Bay Cheese Company
Raw • Microbial coagulant • Farmstead

Sierra Nevada Cheese Company
Pasteurized • Microbial coagulant • Creamery

Siskiyou Crest Goat Dairy
Raw • Microbial coagulant • Farmstead

Spring Hill Cheese Company
Pasteurized • Microbial coagulant • Creamery

Steamboat Island Goat Farm
Raw • Microbial coagulant • Farmstead

FIGARO

Andante Dairy • Petaluma, CA

Moscato d'Asti

Jersey

Mixed herd

Surface-ripened
5 oz. disk
Pasteurized
Microbial coagulant
Affinage of 3 weeks
Available in summer
Creamery
Similar to Robiola Fia

This disk-shaped cheese is only made at the end of California's fig season. The cheese is allowed to develop a thin-skinned rind before it is enveloped in a large fig leaf. The leaf imparts some lively vegetal flavors to the cheese but does not overpower the fresh lactic and wet hay notes. Directly under the rind the paste transforms to a thick liquidy texture, while the inside remains cakey and dense. Figaro is not only an attractive cheese but one that has great complexity of flavor.

FLAGSHEEP

Beecher's Handmade Cheese • Seattle, WA

Pale ale

Jersey and Holstein

Mixed herd

Semi-firm
16 lb. drum
Pasteurized
Microbial coagulant
Affinage of 13 months
Available year-round
Creamery
Similar to Cheddar crossed with Ossau Iraty

The combination of milk (two-thirds cow and one-third sheep) in these clothbound wheels is reflected in the paste's dull yellow hue that becomes darker toward the rind. Unlike other cheeses that go through the cheddaring process, Flagsheep does not flake when cut; the texture is somewhat thick and holds together well when sliced. The aging period is considerable, which gives the secondary cultures time to break down the paste and release earthy sheep notes and lemony flavors

FLAGSHIP

Beecher's Handmade Cheese • Seattle, WA

IPA (Flagship)

Chablis (Flagship Reserve)

Jersey and Holstein

Semi-firm
40 lb. block (Flagship) or
16 lb. drum (Flagship Reserve)
Raw or Pasteurized available
Microbial coagulant
Affinage of 12–18 months
Available year-round
Creamery
Similar to farmhouse Cheddar crossed with young Gouda (Flagship); Similar to farmhouse Cheddar crossed with Gruyère (Flagship Reserve)

Beecher's Handmade Cheese took quite a risk when they developed their first cheese, Flagship, which requires at least twelve months of aging. As the owner recalls, they had to make a year's worth of cheese before they could know, for certain, if their recipe was good. The aim was to move away from grassy, bright flavors in Cheddar and to develop nutty, sweeter flavors, so while the curds are cheddared the cultures added are not Cheddar cultures. Flagship is made in forty-pound blocks and aged out in cryovac packages.

The cheesemaking procedure for the smaller Flagship Reserve wheels is exactly the same as for Flagship until the final step. Instead of going into block-shaped forms, the curds are piled into large, cheesecloth-lined drums. Wrapping or binding wheels in cheesecloth, a traditional practice in the production of English Cheddar, provides a breathable layer of protection for the cheese while still allowing a modest rind to develop. This aging process creates a completely different texture because of the large amount of moisture that comes out of the cheese when the rind is exposed beneath thin cloth rather than protected by a layer of thick plastic. The firm and crumbly paste still retains the desired nutty flavor.

The producers smoke a portion of the blocks to create Smoked Flagship, also aged for a minimum of one year. The flavored riffs on Flagship are both aged just sixty days: No Woman has Pickapeppa Jerk Seasoning mixed into the curds, and Marco Polo is studded with Madagascar peppercorns.

FOG LIGHTS

Cypress Grove Chevre • Arcata, CA

Cabernet franc

Mixed herd

Surface-ripened
8 oz. drum
Pasteurized
Microbial coagulant
Affinage of 3 weeks
Available year-round
Creamery
Similar to aged Selles-sur-Cher

Fog Lights is essentially a miniature version of Humboldt Fog, minus the line of vegetable ash cutting across the paste's center. This cheese was designed to accommodate restaurants or individuals looking for a smaller, more portable wheel of the iconic American original.

FRANKLIN'S RINCONADA TELEME

Midcoast Cheese Company • Los Banos, CA

Chardonnay

Holstein and Jersey

East Friesian–Lacaune cross

Semi-soft
4 lb. square
Pasteurized
Microbial coagulant
Affinage of 10–14 days
Available spring through early summer
Creamery
Similar to Stracchino

The addition of sheep milk to Midcoast Cheese's standard Teleme recipe considerably alters the flavor and even the density of the texture. The sheep milk is sourced from Rinconada Dairy, a nearby farmstead cheesemaker. Franklin's Rinconada Teleme is a bit like the semi-soft sheep wheels made in Spain and Portugal that are characterized by a tacky texture and winey, fermented flavors.

FRANKLIN'S TELEME

Midcoast Cheese Company • Los Banos, CA

Sangiovese

Holstein and Jersey

Semi-soft
6 lb. square
Pasteurized
Microbial coagulant
Affinage of 10–14 days
Available year-round
Creamery
Similar to Stracchino

Cheesemaker Franklin Peluso has kept his family's tradition alive by continuing to produce Teleme cheese, a recipe originally created by his grandfather. To some extent, Teleme is a riff on a style of cheese that has been produced for centuries all over Europe, the most well-known being Italy's Stracchino and Taleggio.

These pudgy squares are made from a fifty-fifty blend of Holstein and Jersey cow milk. The rind doesn't have any molds, instead it gets a dusting of rice flour that keeps the wheels from sticking to shelves and boxes. The off-white paste ranges from semi-soft to gooey as the cheese ages. Flavors of milk, cultured cream, and yeast combine with buttery notes to make the cheese a good candidate for a cheese board and a flavorful addition to pastas and risottos. Peluso also makes a Teleme with crushed black pepper mixed throughout the paste.

FRENCH PRAIRIE

Willamette Valley Cheese Company • Salem, OR

Dry cider

Jersey

Bloomy rind
6 oz. disk
Pasteurized
Microbial coagulant
Affinage of 1 month
Available year-round
Farmstead
Similar to miniature Brie or Camembert

French Prairie is a traditional, disk-shaped, bloomy rind cheese made entirely from the milk of the producer's herd of Jersey cows. *Penicillium candidum* molds develop on the rind and work toward the center, breaking down the paste of the cheese. With carefully monitored temperature and humidity in the aging room, the disks develop over the course of one month until the paste achieves a velvety, smooth texture.

FRESH WITH EWE HINT OF BLUE

Willapa Hills Farmstead Cheese • Doty, WA

German riesling

East Friesian and Lacaune

Blue
5 oz. drum
Pasteurized
Microbial coagulant
Affinage of 3 weeks
Available spring through early fall
Farmstead
Similar to Westfield Blue Log

The cheesemakers at Willapa Hills inoculate sheep milk with a blue mold to make Fresh with Ewe Hint of Blue. Right after coming out of its form it appears identical to the plain, fresh sheep milk cheese that they also produce. But within three weeks, blue-green molds develop on the surface, forming a thin skin that has a slightly sharp flavor. The texture of the paste is cakey and smooth because it still has quite a bit of moisture. Directly beneath the rind, the paste can break down almost to a liquid.

FROMAGE BLANC

The name fromage blanc can imply two different things: the first is a fresh cheese made using lactic coagulation. In this case coagulant is not added to the milk; however, starter bacteria are used to speed up the acidification of the milk just enough so that it forms curds before undesirable flavors develop. The second meaning of fromage blanc is a very fresh, simple cheese where the curds are formed with the addition of a coagulant, drained slightly, and ladled into a mold to develop its shape.

Both versions of fromage blanc made in the United States are pasteurized, have high moisture, light texture, and flavor dominated by tangy acidity. Fromage blanc can be made from whole or skim milk.

Alsea Acre Goat Cheese Farmstead

Appel Farms Farmstead

Beecher's Handmade Cheese Creamery

Bellwether Farms Creamery

Bodega Goat Cheese Farmstead

Cowgirl Creamery Creamery

Cypress Grove Chevre Creamery

Juniper Grove Farm Farmstead

FULL MOON

Rivers Edge Chèvre • Logsden, OR

Champagne

Alpine

Bloomy rind
6–10 oz. disk
Pasteurized
Animal rennet
Affinage of 15 days
Available year-round
Farmstead
Similar to St. Felicien

Rivers Edge makes two versions of this bloomy-rinded wheel: Full Moon is entirely white while Silt Coos is sprinkled with a layer of ash when fresh out of its form, before the bloom is allowed to develop. The younger wheels of each have a cakey center surrounded by some softer paste beneath the rind. As the wheels age, the cakiness is transformed into a creamier texture and eventually can become molten. Both have well-balanced flavors of fresh, clean goat milk, and a touch of tanginess that gives way to peppery flavors with age.

GOAT GOUDA

Central Coast Creamery • Oakdale, CA

IPA

Mixed herd

Semi-soft
9 lb. wheel
Pasteurized
Microbial coagulant
Affinage of 6 months
Available year-round
Creamery
Similar to goat Gouda

Though the recipe is based on classic Gouda, this cheese is unique because it is a larger wheel made entirely from goat milk and because it has some goat cream added. The recipe also includes the acid-reducing step of washing the curds (draining off some of the lactic acid–filled whey and replacing it with water) after the curds have been cut and had a chance to recover. The resulting cheese has a caramely sweetness akin to cooked milk.

Sustainability Spotlight: Bodega Artisan Cheese

Patty Karlin was part of California's back-to-the-land wave in the late 1970s and has been producing goat milk cheeses on her farm in Bodega since 1984. She made weekly deliveries to all of her first customers, natural food stores in Marin, San Francisco, and the East Bay, leaving her farm around eight in the morning and returning in time for lunch; the same trip today would take the better part of a day because of traffic in and out of San Francisco.

Luckily, many things have also changed for the better. Farmers' markets have evolved to become one of Bodega's primary outlets, along with local restaurants whose chefs are devoted to cheeses made by their neighbors. The farm has also gone through a steady transformation as Patty has become more and more interested in the broader meaning of sustainability.

In 2008 Bodega Artisan Cheese began a transition to permaculture. This shift involves planting the farm with shrubs, trees, and ancient grains to become the feed for Patty's goat herd, and creating a garden (fertilized by goat manure) that will be able to feed Patty and other farm workers or volunteers. Patty has plans to create small ridges, or swales, along the hillside acreage of her property that will sequester water for the farm. There is also talk of solar panels for the rooftops of the dairy and her home, which is also located on the farm.

In addition to making cheese since 1984 and her more recent commitment to natural resource projects, Patty has been working to help create business incubators for burgeoning farmers who often face the huge barrier of expensive land prices. As an individual who created an agricultural livelihood for herself, Patty Karlin is passionate about encouraging the next generation of food producers.

GOAT MANCHEGO

Bodega Artisan Cheese • Bodega, CA

Rioja

Alpine

Semi-firm
3 lb. wheel
Raw
Microbial coagulant
Affinage of 2–5 months
Available summer through early winter
Farmstead
Similar to Manchego

As the name implies, the recipe for this cheese is modeled on Manchego though it is made with goat instead of sheep milk. When the freshly formed wheels are unhooped they are flipped frequently to encourage draining. Inside the aging room, the wheels are placed near a fan in an effort to wick moisture away from the surface and encourage a firm rind to develop. The paste has a little grit, like that found in roux, and hearty earth and vegetal flavors.

GOAT TOMME

Laura Chenel's Chevre • Sonoma, CA

Pouilly Fumé

Mixed herd

Semi-firm
3–4 lb. square
Pasteurized
Microbial coagulant
Affinage of 6 months
Available year-round
Creamery
Similar to Malvarosa

This unique, rindless goat milk tomme is formed by wrapping heaps of curds into cloth bags, twisting the loose ends into a knot, and tucking the excess cloth beneath the wheel. The cheeses are left like this overnight, under a press, and then dropped into brine the following day. The wheels are then dried a bit in an haloir (a slightly cool and low humidity room) before they are sealed in bags for aging. The color of the wheels is a striking pure white and the texture is crumbly. Though the paste is sweet like cooked milk, it has a backbone of savory roasted hazelnuts and enough acid to keep the sweeter notes in check.

GOUDA

Belgian

Accounting for more than 60 percent of cheese production in Holland, Goudas can range from mild to sharp depending on the milk type and the length of aging. They are generally subtly sweet and caramel-like early on, developing sharper flavors of coffee, butterscotch, and bittersweet chocolate as they age. Younger wheels have a pliable texture while older wheels are more craggy and firm.

One of the defining qualities of Gouda production is washing the curds after they've been cut. The cheesemaker drains a portion of the whey out of the vat, usually at least one-third if not more, and replaces that drained whey with water. This step removes some of the lactic bacteria (which metabolizes lactose into lactic acid), thereby reducing the development of acidity and contributing to a sweeter flavor and a more pliable texture.

If Goudas are aged beyond six months they can develop small tyrosine crystals, crunchy bits scattered throughout the paste. Goudas are often dipped in wax for the duration of their aging to help the wheels retain moisture.

Appel Farms
Pasteurized • Plain and flavored • Microbial coagulant • Affinage of 2 months • Farmstead

Bravo Farms
Raw • Plain • Microbial coagulant • Affinage of 2–4 months • Creamery

Central Coast Creamery
Pasteurized • Plain • Microbial coagulant • Affinage of 6 months • Creamery

Golden Glen Creamery
Pasteurized • Plain • Microbial coagulant • Affinage of 6 months–4 years • Farmstead

Gothberg Farms
Raw or Pasteurized • Plain • Animal rennet • Affinage of 6 months • Farmstead

Oakdale Cheese
Pasteurized • Plain and flavored • Microbial coagulant • Affinage of 3–12 months • Creamery

Pleasant Valley Dairy
Raw • Plain and flavored • Animal rennet • Affinage varies • Farmstead

Samish Bay Cheese Company
Pasteurized • Plain • Microbial coagulant • Affinage of 2 months–10 years • Farmstead

Winchester Cheese Company
Raw • Plain and flavored • Microbial coagulant • Affinage of 2–12 months • Creamery

GOUDA

Pleasant Valley Dairy • Ferndale, WA

Syrah

Mixed herd

Semi-soft
2 lb. or 6 lb. wheel
Raw
Animal rennet
Affinage of 2 months
Available year-round
Farmstead
Similar to Gouda

Pleasant Valley Dairy has been making farmstead Gouda since the mid-1970s. These wheels are consistently springy in texture and, when young, they are sometimes a bit crumbly toward the center. The flavor of the paste is reminiscent of buttermilk, but the acidity is tempered by nutty flavors. Occasionally the wheels have hints of spring onion flavors. Gouda is a mainstay at Pleasant Valley; they also produce a range of flavored Goudas and a well-balanced, delicately smoked version that does not overpower the flavors of the cheese.

GOUDA

Winchester Cheese Company • Winchester, CA

Brown ale

Holstein

Semi-firm
11–12 lb. wheel
Raw
Microbial coagulant
Affinage of 2–12 months
Available year-round
Creamery
Similar to traditional Gouda

Winchester Cheese's founder, Jules Wesselink, was raised in Holland and has recreated the cheeses of his home country in California's Central Valley. Having sold their 500 Holsteins, they are no longer farmstead, though they continue to work with neighboring farms to obtain high-quality Holstein milk for cheesemaking. Jules has since retired but Winchester continues to make Gouda in a variety of ages starting with Mild Gouda, aged just two months. Medium Gouda is aged from three to six months and has a lactic caramel flavor and a soft, bendy texture. Sharp Gouda, aged a minimum of six months, has a light body that flakes apart and melts on the tongue. The Sharp wheels taste of toast and toasted nuts and the paste is dotted with crunchy tyrosine crystals. Small amounts of reserved Super Aged Gouda are aged a minimum of one year. Winchester also produces some flavored varieties of Gouda most of which are aged for two months.

GRANDE ROSA

Blue Rose Dairy • Winlock, WA

Dolcetto

Primarily Saanen and Alpine

Fresh
5–8 lb. wheel
Pasteurized
Animal rennet
Affinage of 1–2 days
Available year-round
Farmstead
Similar to loaf mozzarella

The curds of this tall wheel are not stretched during production but the texture of the paste is similar to a pasta filata-style cheese. The paste has a springy texture and simple, clean lactic flavors. Wheels are made entirely from goat milk and have a natural, bright white rind because the affinage is so short and the cheese is protected by a plastic wrapping.

GRAVENSTEIN GOLD

Redwood Hill Farm • Sebastopol, CA

Dry cider

Alpine, LaMancha, Nubian, and Saanen

Washed rind
3–4 lb. wheel
Raw
Microbial coagulant
Affinage of 2 months
Available in fall
Creamery
Kosher and Certified Humane Raised and Handled
Similar to Chimay

This is the first washed rind offering from one of the founding farms in the world of California goat cheese. Gravenstein apple cider is used to wash the cheese since Redwood Hill Farm is situated in prime Gravenstein apple country. The rinds of these goat milk tommes turn a burnt peach color as a result of the repeated washings during their two to four months of aging. The paste maintains a hearty, herbaceous quality along with pungent flavors coming from the rind. Depending on the exact age of the wheels, they range from chalky at the center to pudgy throughout.

GRISDALE GOAT

Estrella Family Creamery • Montesano, WA

Blauer Zweigelt

Primarily LaMancha

Semi-soft
2 lb. wheel
Raw
Animal rennet
Affinage of 2 months
Available spring through fall
Farmstead
Similar to Garrotxa

When cut in half, the cross sections of these wheels are shaped like boomerangs. The curds are hand-pressed in cheesecloth. Then the edges of the cloth are knotted up and the cheese is set on top of it, resulting in a big indentation on the underside of the finished wheel. A rough, natural rind develops that is mottled brown and gray. The paste is earthy and smooth carrying its goaty qualities through to the sweet toffee finish.

GUAPIER

Estrella Family Creamery • Montesano, WA

Madeira

Primarily Normandy

Semi-soft
4–4.5 lb. wheel
Raw
Animal rennet
Affinage of 3–4 months
Available year-round
Farmstead
Similar to Morbier

The Estrellas make cheese every morning and afternoon as they do not have a bulk tank to hold milk. Guapier is made in exactly the same way as the French cheese Morbier. In the morning, a layer of curd is placed into the molds, followed by a layer of ash. Then it waits until a second layer of curd—from the evening milking—is laid over the top. The supple but firm orange- and rust-colored rind shows evidence of the washing it undergoes during development. The paste has a brilliant lactic flavor and a creamy, springy texture.

HANNAH BRIDGE

Ancient Heritage Dairy • Scio, OR

Dry riesling

Ayrshire and Guernsey

East Friesian–Lacaune cross

Semi-firm
5 lb. wheel
Raw
Animal rennet
Affinage of 2 months
Available summer through winter
Farmstead
Similar to young Appenzeller

The dark brown hue of Hannah Bridge's rind comes from cocoa that is rubbed on the exterior during the aging process. The semi-firm texture of this mixed milk cheese is creamier than if the cheese was made only with cow's milk. Though at first seeming to come on strong, the earthy, fermented flavors typical of mountain-style cheeses are restrained. The finish is a combination of milky and rustic notes.

HARVEST

Rivers Edge Chèvre • Logsden, OR

Albariño

Alpine

Fresh
6–7 oz. ball
Pasteurized
Animal rennet
Affinage of 4–5 days
Available in fall
Farmstead
Similar to chèvre

Harvest is a clever, seasonal, fresh goat milk cheese molded into a pumpkin shape and colored orange-red with paprika. The crowning touch is the maple vine attached to the top which acts as the pumpkin's stem.

HAVARTI

Amber ale

Havarti is a traditional Danish cow's milk cheese which has prominent flavors of butter and a slight yeasty sweetness. During production the curds are washed, making the cheese milder. Rind development does not occur on the wheels; they are either brined or aged in plastic to inhibit mold growth. Havarti melts well due to its moderate moisture content and springy curds.

Loleta Cheese Factory
Pasteurized • Plain and flavored • Microbial coagulant • Creamery

Pine Stump Farms
Raw • Plain • Microbial coagulant • Farmstead

Willamette Valley Cheese Company
Pasteurized • Plain and flavored • Microbial coagulant • Farmstead

HERBS IN BLOOM

Estrella Family Creamery • Montesano, WA

Old world pinot noir

Primarily Normandy

Bloomy rind
I lb. wheel
Raw
Animal rennet
Affinage of 2 months
Available year-round
Farmstead
Similar to Fleur du Maquis

Though made from cow milk, this herb-encrusted wheel is reminiscent of a Corsican sheep milk cheese called Fleur du Maquis. The small tommes have a pudgy interior, often becoming a tad firmer and pock-marked toward the center. Each wheel is covered in fennel pollen and lavender, which transmit subtle floral and herbal flavors into the cheese. The paste is salty and lactic, like a balanced cultured butter, and the texture is silky on the palate.

HILLIS PEAK

Pholia Farm • Rogue River, OR

Riesling

Nigerian Dwarf

Semi-firm
2.5 lb. drum
Raw
Microbial coagulant
Affinage of 6 months
Available year-round
Farmstead
Similar to Ibores

The rind of Hillis Peak, a washed-curd, lightly pressed tomme, is rubbed with oil and paprika during aging to give it a deep reddish-brown hue. The paste is quite firm but becomes creamy on the palate. Flavors range from cooked milk sweetness to a mineral, wet rock note directly beneath the rind. The finish is smooth, dominated by a dusty earthiness.

HUMBOLDT FOG

Cypress Grove Chèvre • Arcata, CA

Gamay

Mixed herd

Surface-ripened
1 lb. or 5 lb. wheel
Pasteurized
Microbial coagulant
Affinage of 3 weeks
Available year-round
Creamery
Similar to aged Valençay

When cheesemaker Mary Keehn was asked how she developed Humboldt Fog she replied, "it came to me in a dream." After this inspired dream (which took place on a plane returning from Europe) Keehn rushed home to her cheese plant to make the cheese, which has since become one of the most iconic American cheeses on the market.

The wheel's size and height, combined with a delicate white rind over a dusting of black ash, makes this cheese resemble a cake. The paste, both light in texture and dense with moisture on the palate, is cut through the center with a dark line of vegetable ash. These wheels require a mere three weeks to mature though they can develop for additional weeks without deteriorating.

HYKU

Goat's Leap • Saint Helena, CA

Pinot gris

LaMancha

Surface-ripened
6–8 oz. disk
Pasteurized
Animal rennet
Affinage of 7–10 days
Available year-round
Farmstead
Similar to Pélardon

The petite size and relatively large surface area makes for a rapid ripening of these wrinkled-bloom, goat cheese disks. The interior becomes dense and smooth while maintaining the bright and tangy flavors of a young goat milk cheese.

ILAHEE TOMME

Rivers Edge Chèvre • Logsden, OR

Old world pinot noir

Alpine

Semi-firm
2 lb. wheel
Raw
Animal rennet
Affinage of 5 months
Available year-round
Farmstead
Similar to Capra Valtellina

Ilahee Tomme is hard to come by since its affinage is labor intensive. Curds are gradually scooped from the vat into forms, and pressed and turned repeatedly to expel moisture. Once out of their forms they are smoked slightly and then rubbed regularly throughout their development with a combination of olive and truffle oils. Wheels remain in the aging room for a minimum of five months and develop a firm, smooth texture, and a balance of savory and nutty flavors.

IMPROMPTU

Andante Dairy • Petaluma, CA

Banyuls

Jersey

Mixed herd

Hard
Size and shape varies
Pasteurized
Microbial coagulant
Affinage of 6 months
Availability varies
Creamery
Similar to rustic pecorino

A true cheesemaker's cheese, the spur-of-the-moment Impromptu is only made when there is an overabundance of milk. Since it is designed to utilize surplus, this cheese can be any combination of the cow and goat milk used by Soyoung Scanlan. The affinage varies greatly, likely depending on the milk ratio and components, though all of the wheels are aged at least six months and have a dry, flakey texture. Impromptu is made using techniques of cheesemakers in the Pyrenees and thus shares rich, toasted nut and sweet toffee flavors that characterize the cheeses of that region.

10 INVERNESS

Cowgirl Creamery • Petaluma, CA

Champagne

Holstein, Jersey,
and Holstein–Jersey cross

Surface-ripened
3 oz. column
Pasteurized
Microbial coagulant
Affinage of 10 days
Available year-round
Creamery
Certified Organic
Similar to Robiola

Inverness is reminiscent of Italian Robiola-style cheeses that are made in an array of shapes and variety of milk types throughout the Piedmont region of Italy. This delicate surface-ripened cheese is only available at Cowgirl Creamery's retail locations. Made with certified organic milk from a local herd of Jerseys and Holsteins, the cheese has a light, pillowy interior, and earthy flavors of wet hay and barnyard crossed with a lively tang.

ITALIAN STYLE TABLE CHEESE

Vella Cheese Company • Sonoma, CA

Sangiovese

Holstein and Guernsey

Semi-soft
10 lb. wheel
Raw
Microbial coagulant
Affinage of 2 months
Available year-round
Creamery
Similar to fontina

At the time Vella Cheese Company began making this cheese, modeled after Italy's fontina, buyers at various grocery outlets informed them that they were not allowed to call it Fontina. They were encouraged to name it Fontinella but everyone else in the industry was already doing that, so Vella went a different route and called it Italian Style Table Cheese. The wheels are off-white in color and do not develop much of a rind. The cheese looks softer than it actually is, and though the texture appears dry when cut it becomes fudgy on the tongue. The paste has bright, winey flavors, a hint of brown butter, and a bite on the finish.

JACK

Lager

Jack cheese is also sometimes called Monterey Jack because it was created in Monterey, CA. This semi-soft cheese has flavors reminiscent of salted cultured butter. Jack can be made in blocks and aged in plastic, like block Cheddar, or made in wheel form. Either way, it usually does not have a natural rind.

Beecher's Handmade Cheese
Pasteurized • Plain and flavored • Microbial coagulant • Creamery

Bravo Farms
Raw • Flavored • Microbial coagulant • Creamery

Loleta Cheese Factory
Pasteurized • Plain and flavored • Microbial coagulant • Creamery

Rumiano Cheese Company
Pasteurized • Plain and flavored • Microbial coagulant • Creamery

Sierra Nevada Cheese Company
Pasteurized • Plain and flavored (cow milk only) • Microbial coagulant • Creamery

Spring Hill Cheese Company
Pasteurized • Plain and flavored • Microbial coagulant • Creamery

Steamboat Island Goat Farm
Raw • Plain and flavored • Microbial coagulant • Farmstead

Vella Cheese Company
Pasteurized • Plain and flavored • Microbial coagulant • Creamery

Willamette Valley Cheese Company
Pasteurized • Plain • Microbial coagulant • Farmstead

10 JUPITER MOON

Rivers Edge Chèvre • Logsden, OR

Oloroso sherry

Alpine

Washed rind
16 oz. disk
Pasteurized
Animal rennet
Affinage of 1–2 months
Available year-round
Farmstead
Similar to Vacherin Mont d'Or

There is a lot going on in these low-lying disks. The curds are first washed to control acidity and make the texture of the cheese pudgier. After coming out of their forms, the wheels are washed with a mixture of sherry from Madrone Mountain (a local producer of dessert wines) and brine. Then each wheel is bound around its edge with a spruce band. Aromas of apricots, woodsy goat milk, and musky cellar permeate the paste. The texture is smooth and a bit clay-like. On the palate, the earthiness comes through along with goat butter flavors.

KIKU

Goat's Leap • Saint Helena, CA

Quincy

LaMancha

Surface-ripened
3–4 oz. disk
Pasteurized
Animal rennet
Affinage of 3 weeks
Available in summer
Farmstead
Similar to Robiola Fia

The cheesemaker named this cheese Kiku because she enjoyed the sound of the word, even though it means chrysanthemum in Japanese. These petite diskettes are wrapped in fig leaves that have been macerated in sauvignon blanc. The paste has all the flavors associated with slightly aged goat milk cheeses (tangy, fresh) with the addition of some tropical notes. The texture, over time, will transform from cakey to thick and creamy.

KILLEEN

Estrella Family Creamery • Montesano, WA

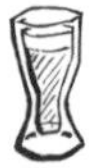

Brown ale

Primarily Normandy

Primarily LaMancha

Semi-firm
5 lb. wheel
Raw
Animal rennet
Affinage of 2 months
Available summer through mid-fall
Farmstead
Similar to Bra Tenero

Kelli Estrella only makes this cheese in the spring when the cows get their first access to young shoots of grass and their milk takes on a rich, golden hue. The brightly colored milk is critical to the stunning visual and flavorful aspects of this cheese. The paste is constructed with two layers of cow milk curd with a streak of goat milk curd running through the middle. The contrast of the lactic, unctuous cow milk against the refreshing, woodsy goat milk makes for a long finish. The cheese has a somewhat open texture, pocked with small, uneven holes. Wheels develop a natural rind that is wiped down regularly to discourage mold growth.

LADYSMITH

Samish Bay Cheese Company • Bow, WA

Chenin blanc

Jersey, Milking Shorthorn,
and Jersey–Milking Shorthorn cross

Semi-soft
1 lb. or 2 lb. wheel
Pasteurized
Microbial coagulant
1–2 days (fresh), 2–3 weeks (aged)
Available year-round
Farmstead
Certified Organic
Similar to fresh Toma

These wheels are so fresh-flavored that they taste like curds that have barely knitted together. Soft and springy in texture, the paste has an intense fresh cheese acidity and a dominant sweet cream butter flavor. Ladysmith comes in two ages: the younger, fresh wheels are kept just a couple of days, and the older wheels are held until they form a hint of a rind which takes about two to three weeks. This cheese would be a lovely addition to a breakfast board accompanied by plum preserves.

LA JERSEY

Silver Springs Creamery • Lyndon, WA

Lager

Jersey

Mixed herd

Semi-soft
10 lb. wheel
Pasteurized
Animal rennet
Affinage of 2 months
Available year-round
Creamery
Similar to young Gouda

The bright white goat milk in this cheese comes from a neighboring farm and is bolstered by the addition of rich, yellow-hued milk from the producer's four Jersey cows. Combining these two milks boosts the volume of cheese, and also yields a creamy texture. To prevent the development of mold on the rind during aging, each wheel is painted with a lightweight, breathable coating once they've finished draining.

LA PANZA GOLD

Rinconada Dairy • Santa Margarita, CA

Vin Santo

East Friesian–Lacaune cross

Semi-firm
2 lb. wheel
Raw
Animal rennet
Affinage of 2 months
Available late spring through fall
Farmstead
Similar to Corsican sheep tomme

La Panza Gold is modeled after some Corsican sheep cheeses but also shares characteristics with sheep tommes produced in the Pyrenees. The rind's rich brown color is partially a result of the wheels having been washed in whey. The paste is semi-firm and has a range of flavors—a hint of olives and meatiness on the savory side is balanced by brown butter notes. Some wheels are released as early as two months but many are stocked away and held until they are a few months older. La Panza Gold is delicious paired with fresh figs or dates.

LARGO

Andante Dairy • Petaluma, CA

Nebbiolo

Jersey

Surface-ripened
1 lb. wheel with sloped sides
Pasteurized
Microbial coagulant
Affinage of 1 month
Available year-round
Creamery
Similar to Fleur-de-Lis

The shape of this triple cream cheese is a small, truncated cone with delicately sloped sides. It has a crinkly rind often found on small semi-aged cheeses from Italy's Piedmont region and on the little goat cheeses of France. Largo can thank the combination of whole Jersey cow milk and crème fraîche for its luscious texture. This mild and flavorful cheese combines lactic flavors (similar to cream cheese), a bit of barnyard funk, and a good dose of salt. Largo is also made in a miniature six- to seven- ounce size called Picolo, which is aged only two weeks.

LARKHAVEN AUTUMN GOATLING

Larkhaven Farmstead Cheese • Tonasket, WA

Sweet riesling

Mixed herd

Surface-ripened
12 oz. disk
Raw
Animal rennet
Affinage of 2–3 months
Available summer through early winter
Farmstead
Similar to Banon

Late-season goat milk and the boon of autumn's maple leaves are celebrated in this cheese. Each disk of Larkhaven Autumn Goatling is aged slightly to allow for the development of a thin, crinkled skin before being wrapped in the leaves. The vegetal, earthy notes are a combination of the natural flavor development of the cheese and the interaction of the cheese with the surrounding leaf. Because of the small size of this cheese, when it is aged for as long as three months it can lose a lot of moisture, firming up the paste considerably.

LARKHAVEN GOATLING

Larkhaven Farmstead Cheese • Tonasket, WA

Red ale

Mixed herd

Washed rind
12 oz. disk
Raw
Animal rennet
Affinage of 2–3 months
Available late fall through winter
Farmstead
Similar to chevrotin

The petite size of this cheese increases the paste's potential to break down throughout the two- to three-month affinage. Made entirely from raw goat milk, these disks are washed regularly during their development to activate the bacteria on their rinds. These bacteria, working to break down fats and proteins, are also responsible for the rusty-orange hue of the rind. The paste can range from chalky at the center of younger wheels to dense and smooth in those that have aged longer.

LARZAC

Monteillet Fromagerie • Dayton, WA

Viognier

Alpine

Surface-ripened
8–10 oz. sloped drum
Pasteurized
Microbial coagulant
Affinage of 10–14 days
Available spring through fall
Farmstead
Similar to Robiola

The production of Larzac involves taking curds that look almost like chèvre and packing them into slightly sloped cylindrical forms. Halfway up, a layer of vegetable ash is sprinkled, and then the form is filled with more curds. The cheese is left to sit like this overnight so that the curds will knit together. Then each piece can be turned onto a metal rack where the rinds will dry off just enough to begin to develop a thin skin. After a full week in the aging room the paste becomes dense and rich, filled with rustic flavors of damp hay and fresh goat milk.

LEGATO

Andante Dairy • Petaluma, CA

Prosecco

Jersey

Bloomy rind
4.5 oz. disk
Pasteurized
Microbial coagulant
Affinage of 3 weeks
Available year-round
Creamery
Similar to Camembert

The recipe for Legato is modeled after France's famous Camembert. The curds are cut into large pieces and ladled into molds to drain. After salting, the disks are allowed three weeks to develop downy white rinds. Each cheese is flipped regularly to ensure even rind development and to keep moisture within the paste from collecting on one side of the cheese. The high-fat content Jersey milk used to make this cheese is evident in the thick and gooey texture of the paste.

LE ROI

Monteillet Fromagerie • Dayton, WA

Jura

Alpine

Surface-ripened
3 oz. disk
Pasteurized
Microbial coagulant
Affinage of 2 weeks
Available spring through fall
Farmstead
Similar to St. Felicien

Le Roi (the king) is fittingly topped with a flourish of pure, edible gold dust. This flat, round disk is covered on the outside with grape leaf ash, and the contrast of the bone-white paste against the charcoal gray rind is visually stunning. The full two-week affinage is enough time to break the interior down into an unctuous paste. Although Le Roi is small in size it is big in flavor: funky vegetal crossed with rich, goat milk notes.

LIONZA

Fiscalini Farmstead Cheese Company • Modesto, CA

 ***New world sauvignon blanc***

 ***Holstein***

Semi-firm
26 lb. wheel
Raw
Microbial coagulant
Affinage of 6 months
Available year-round
Farmstead
Validus Certified Responsible Producer
Similar to Abondance

Owner John Fiscalini and cheesemaker Mariano Gonzalez traveled to Switzerland to learn how to make a cheese in the style of the regional homeland of John's family. The paste of this large wheel has a firm texture that becomes smooth on the palate. Lionza has classic mountain cheese flavors, a subtle hint of hazelnuts, and notes of mild tropical fruit which grow stronger toward the finish.

Sustainability Spotlight: Fiscalini Farmstead Cheese Company

John Fiscalini is a third generation dairy farmer whose grandfather had the foresight, in 1914, to purchase land in what is now one of the world's prime agricultural regions, the San Joaquin Valley. The farm was originally a pasture-based operation but gradually the Fiscalinis migrated to a confinement operation because they found it to be cleaner and more efficient.

Two of John's three children expressed interest in being part of the business but because the dairy had become so efficient, it was hard for John to foresee enough work for two additional staff. Around this time, the California Milk Advisory Board offered courses on becoming a farmstead cheesemaker and John attended with great curiosity. In late 2000, Fiscalini added a cheesemaking facility to their dairy farm and began working on recipes. The following year, celebrated cheesemaker Mariano Gonzalez came to work for the Fiscalinis as their Master Cheesemaker and helped them develop award-winning Cheddar and mountain-style cheeses.

One of the most interesting aspects of the business is John's focus on sustainability. In 2009, John completed construction of a massive anaerobic digester that breaks down waste from his herd of 3000 cows. A major byproduct of the digester is methane, which John captures, cools, cleanses, and uses as energy to power and heat water for the dairy and cheese plant.

LITTLE BOY BLUE

Willapa Hills Farmstead Cheese • Doty, WA

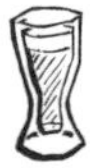

English ale

Jersey and Holstein

Blue
1 lb. drum
Raw
Animal rennet
Affinage of 2 months
Available year-round
Creamery
Similar to Cashel Blue

This compact, natural-rinded, blue cheese is made with unpasteurized milk from Jerseys and Holsteins. The combination of milk types gives the paste a thick texture. While the paste is somewhat creamy, it is lower in moisture than other blues so it is a bit bendy and less buttery. Little Boy Blue's dusty, earthy, blue mold flavor, and underlying notes of hay are broken up by a slight bitterness similar to that found in bittersweet chocolate.

MARY'S PEAK

Rivers Edge Chèvre • Logsden, OR

Sancerre

Alpine

Surface-ripened
4.5–5 oz. pyramid
Pasteurized
Animal rennet
Affinage of 15 days
Available year-round
Farmstead
Similar to Pouligny-Saint-Pierre

A riff on a French classic, Mary's Peak has a velvety white rind (developed by *Geotrichum* yeasts) instead of the wrinkly skin typical of pyramid-shaped Pouligny-Saint-Pierre. Cheesemaker Patricia Morford also makes Cape Foulweather, another version of this pyramid that is sprinkled with a layer of ash prior to the development of the bloomy rind. Humbug Mountain is a third, slightly varied form that looks like a pyramid whose top has been lopped off. All three cheeses have spicy, briney flavors and a light texture when they are younger. If aged longer, they can evolve to become piquant in flavor and smooth in texture.

MASCARPONE

Pronounced mah-scah-poane, this traditional, fresh Italian cheese is made by gently coagulating cream with an acid or starter culture to help increase the acidity. Using an acid speeds up the process and can result in a thicker end product. If a culture is used for the coagulation, the cream and culture must be left to set overnight and then can be drained to the desired thickness.

Mascarpone is often used in pastries and is also a lovely accompaniment to fresh berries and other summer fruits.

Belfiore Cheese Company Creamery

Gioia Cheese Company Creamery

Jacobs Creamery Creamery

MAYOR OF NYE BEACH

Rivers Edge Chèvre • Logsden, OR

Calvados

Alpine

Washed rind
16–20 oz. square
Raw
Animal rennet
Affinage of 2 months
Available year-round
Farmstead
Similar to Maroilles

These handsome squares are made from curds that have been washed, a step that creates slightly sweeter and more pliable curds. Once popped out of their forms, the squares are washed with neighbor Siletz Brewery's Spruce Tips Ale and brine so that they develop a pale orange-brown rind and the paste begins to soften. The flavor is brawny and earthy with hints of pine nuts.

Craft Spotlight: Rivers Edge Chèvre

Goats have been a part of Pat Morford's life since she was a small girl drinking fresh goat milk and eating simple homemade cheeses. Having animals to provide milk for her family was always a way of living that made sense to her, but it wasn't until Pat and her partner, George, moved to their farm in Logsden, near the Oregon coast, that she considered keeping a larger herd of animals. Pat developed a sturdy herd of goats and attempted to sell milk to a nearby cow dairy but the economics weren't right; meanwhile, George's work as a commercial fisherman was drying up.

Pat and George decided to take the plunge into farmstead cheesemaking and began collecting equipment. Once construction on the milking parlor and creamery were completed, Pat started making a range of goat milk cheeses, from fresh chèvre and bloomy rinds to aged tomes. All varieties of cheese made by Pat and her daughters, who have helped her in the creamery since the beginning, have pure flavors that come from clean, carefully handled milk. The success of Rivers Edge is a testament to the knowledge Pat has acquired over a lifetime spent caring for and working with goats.

Pat's familiarity with the flavors and textures that can come from goat milk is shown in the rapid evolution of her line of cheeses. Bloomy rind and surface-ripened have been some of the most challenging styles of cheese for American producers because the affinage required is difficult and the historical knowledge or information available about aging these types of cheese are limited. Pat has shown determination to master these styles and her committed customers are proof that she is headed in that direction. The cheeses are entirely handcrafted, all the way down to the labels that Pat illustrated years ago which are still attached to every piece of cheese that is made on the farm.

MEJEAN

Monteillet Fromagerie • Dayton, WA

Grenache

East Friesian and Lacaune

Surface-ripened
8–10 oz. disk
Pasteurized
Microbial coagulant
Affinage of 3 weeks
Available late spring through early fall
Farmstead
Similar to Pérail

The Monteillets modeled this cheese after a well-known French favorite called Pérail. Each disk develops a skin-textured rind on its surface that breaks down the 100 percent sheep milk paste below. When young, the inside of the cheese is fresh and fluffy becoming more luscious and runny as it ages. Throughout its development the flavors shift from fresh and acidic to funkier vegetal notes of damp hay.

MÉLANGE

Andante Dairy • Petaluma, CA

Arneis

Jersey

Mixed herd

Surface-ripened
4–5 oz. disk, 5–6 oz. pyramid, 8 oz. square
Pasteurized
Microbial coagulant
Affinage of 2 weeks
Available year-round
Creamery
Similar to La Tur

This cheese, made from a mixture of cow and goat milk, comes in three shapes: a petite disk (Round), a tall pyramid (Metronome), and a small square (Pave). The smooth texture is velvety without being heavy. Hints of damp hay and briney tang balance the dominant fresh cream flavor and give this cheese an edge. In addition to the variety of shapes, the cheesemaker has also created two more versions of the disk: Rondo has an herb-dusted rind, and Cadenza is covered in post-harvest pomace from two of Sonoma County's best-known wine varietals, syrah and pinot noir.

MEZZO SECCO

Vella Cheese Company • Sonoma, CA

Nebbiolo

Holstein and Guernsey

Hard
10 lb. wheel
Raw
Microbial coagulant
Affinage of 5 months
Available year-round
Creamery
Similar to Grana Padano

Back in the days before refrigeration, this seasonal cheese was created to endure the warmer months when there wasn't enough room to fit cheese on the ice block in addition to milk and butter. Mezzo Secco, half-dry, is basically a jack cheese with less moisture. The paste smells like browned butter and some of that nuttiness comes through in the flavor, along with tropical fruit notes and a slight bite on the finish. Vella ages some wheels of Mezzo Secco even longer (two years minimum) and calls them Oro Secco, dry gold. Oro Secco has a drier texture, studded with small crystals, and tastes of butterscotch.

MINUET

Andante Dairy • Petaluma, CA

Muscadet

Jersey

Mixed herd

Surface-ripened
8 oz. drum
Pasteurized
Microbial coagulant
Affinage of 3 weeks
Available year-round
Creamery
Similar to Explorateur

The unique combination of goat milk and cow milk cream is evident in the initial citrusy, lactic flavors that give way to a gentler finish. Formed into a squat column and enveloped by a powdery white rind, the paste of Minuet is thick directly beneath the rind and gets fluffier at the center.

MONET TORTE

Harley Farms • Pescadero, CA

Sancerre

American Alpine

Fresh
3 oz. or 7 oz. disk
Pasteurized
Microbial coagulant
Affinage of 3–4 days
Available year-round
Farmstead
Similar to chèvre

Though Monet Torte is indeed a fresh goat cheese, the act of placing it in shaped molds and pressing edible flowers and herbs into its surface distinguishes it from other chèvre. Dee Harley, the owner and cheesemaker at Harley Farms, milks more than 200 American Alpine goats at her farm on the California coast. These wheels of decorated chèvre are mild in flavor and dense in texture, allowing the herbs to stand out on the palate.

MONTASIO

Samish Bay Cheese Company • Bow, WA

Brown ale

Jersey, Milking Shorthorn, and Jersey–Milking Shorthorn cross

Semi-firm
1 lb., 2 lb., or 6–8 lb. wheel
Raw
Microbial coagulant
Affinage of 3 months
Available year-round
Farmstead
Certified Organic
Similar to Italian Montasio

Samish Bay uses certified organic milk from their herd to create a distinct version of Montasio, an Italian cheese named for its region of production in the Montasio Alps. During cheesemaking, the curds are cooked to expel moisture and create a smooth texture. The wheels are sealed before being aged; this prohibits the majority of rind formation though wheels still become covered, over time, with small, white calcium crystals. Reserve wheels of Montasio are cellared at Samish Bay for up to ten years. During aging these wheels develop assertive vegetal notes and a sharp finish that lingers.

MOPSY'S BEST

Black Sheep Creamery • Adna, WA

Sangiovese

East Friesian and Lacaune

Semi-firm
3–3.5 lb. wheel
Raw
Microbial coagulant
Affinage of 3 months
Available summer through early winter
Farmstead
Similar to young pecorino

Modeled after aged British sheep cheeses, this farmstead tomme displays the kind of richness expected in semi-firm cheeses made entirely from sheep milk. Mopsy's Best has a minimum affinage of three months, during which it develops a lean sharpness that is subtler than a Pecorino Romano but gives the paste a depth of flavor. This cheese becomes creamy on the palate and pairs well with quince paste, also known as membrillo.

MOUNTAIN TOMME

Alpine Lakes Sheep Cheese • Leavenworth, WA

Chardonnay

East Friesian and Lacaune with genetics from fiber sheep breeds

Semi-firm
3–5 lb. wheel
Raw
Microbial coagulant
Affinage of 2 months
Available late summer through spring
Farmstead
Similar to Vermont Shepherd

Showcasing classic sheep milk flavors, Mountain Tomme is modeled on a well-loved sheep milk tomme produced by Vermont Shepherd Farm in Putney, Vermont. The rind is different from Vermont Shepherd's because the cheesemaker dips the wheels in black wax for the duration of their aging. The wheels are lightly pressed with small, two-pound weights, and the paste of the cheese is a bit dry but comes together nicely on the palate. An underlying sweet flavor, similar to almonds or almond milk, is balanced by earthy notes. Mountain Tomme would make a wonderful accompaniment to an aperitif, alongside olives and marcona almonds.

MOZZARELLA

Lambrusco

Mozzarella is part of a large family of cheeses called formaggio di pasta filata, meaning paste that threads. All of the cheeses in this family (including caciocavallo, provolone, and scamorza) are produced by stretching or pulling the curds. Once the curds have been cut they are heated slightly, this encourages a rise in acidity which makes the curds clump together and become fibrous yet elastic. At this point the cheesemaker slices pieces off the mass of curd and puts them in hot water or hot whey (approximately 170 degrees F) so that they soften up and can be pulled like taffy. The curds are removed from the water, stretched until they have reached the proper consistency, and formed into a variety of shapes. Today many producers use machines to stretch and shape the curds because stretching and forming each piece by hand is labor intensive and less consistent.

Some of the most common shapes are ciliegini (little cherries, approximately one-third ounce), nodini (knot-shape, approximately one ounce), bocconcini (little mouthfuls, one and a half ounces), and ovolini (egg-shape, approximately four ounces). Most often the terms mozzarella and fior di latte are used to describe a larger size which ranges from eight to twelve ounces.

Mozzarella was traditionally made with milk from water buffalo and still is by some producers. The buffalo milk gives the cheese an earthier, slightly musky flavor while mozzarella made from cow milk tastes fresh and milky. Today, mozzarella made from cow milk is labeled fior di latte in Italy. Classic accompaniments to any fresh mozzarella are cured meats, or sliced tomatoes with basil leaves, a touch of olive oil, and a sprinkle of sea salt.

Belfiore Cheese Company
Mozzarella, fior di latte, and bocconcini • Microbial coagulant • Creamery

Bubalus Bubalis
Mozzarella and bocconcini • Microbial coagulant • Creamery

Fiscalini Farmstead Cheese Company
Ovolini, bocconcini, and ciliegini • Microbial coagulant • Farmstead

Gioia Cheese Company
Ovolini, nodini, bocconcini, and ciliegini • Microbial coagulant • Creamery

Golden Glen Creamery
Mozzarella • Microbial coagulant • Farmstead

River Valley Cheese
Mozzarella • Microbial coagulant • Farmstead

Samish Bay Cheese Company
Mozzarella • Microbial coagulant • Farmstead

MOZZARELLA DI BUFALA

Bubalus Bubalis • Gardenia, CA

Lambrusco

Water Buffalo

Fresh
8 oz. ball
Pasteurized
Microbial coagulant
No affinage
Available year-round
Creamery
Similar to Mozzarella di Bufala

The flavor in the buffalo milk mozzarella from Bubalus Bubalis is yeasty and slightly gamey unlike the sweeter, milky flavor of cow milk mozzarella (also called fior di latte), which represents the majority of mozzarella produced in the United States. Mozzarella was originally developed in Italy with buffalo milk and producers only began using cow milk when there was not enough buffalo milk to sustain the demand. The balls of Mozzarella di Bufala are plump with moisture and have a slightly grainy texture. This cheese is always the perfect accompaniment to ripe tomatoes and fresh basil.

MT. TAM

Cowgirl Creamery • Petaluma, CA

Syrah

Holstein, Jersey, and Holstein–Jersey cross

Bloomy rind
10 oz. drum
Pasteurized
Microbial coagulant
Affinage of 1 month
Available year-round
Creamery
Certified Organic
Similar to Camembert crossed with Saint André

Mt.Tam was developed by Cowgirl Creamery's first cheesemaker who was from Holland and heavily influenced by Dutch cheeses (like Gouda), the production of which often involves washing the curds. Washed curd, bloomy rind cheeses do exist but they are not very common. In the case of Mt. Tam, washing the curds after cutting them slows down the acidification and creates a more elastic texture and sweeter flavor. Once the curds are pumped into their forms they sit for an hour and a half before being flipped and left overnight in the cheese room. The following day they are placed in a brine tank which adds salt to the cheese, for flavor purposes, and slows bacterial activity. The resulting cheese develops a thick, lush, and slightly tacky interior, and prominent flavors of fresh butter, earth, and mushrooms.

MUTSCHLI

Pleasant Valley Dairy • Ferndale, WA

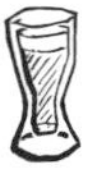

Belgian ale

Mixed herd

Semi-firm
2 lb. or 6 lb. wheel
Raw
Animal rennet
Affinage of 2 months
Available year-round
Farmstead
Similar to Raclette

The cheesemaker at Pleasant Valley says this cheese looks like "Swiss without the holes." As with all cheeses made at Pleasant Valley, the Mutschli comes in two sizes. Young wheels, which can be sold as early as two months, taste slightly pungent and lactic, like the French mountain-style cheese Raclette. The flavors ripen and the paste firms up considerably as the wheels continue to age. Some wheels are aged out to two years and the paste hardens to the point where it crumbles like Parmesan.

MUTSCHLI

Rosecrest Farm • Chehalis, WA

Belgian ale

Milking Shorthorns

Semi-firm
3.5 lb. wheel
Raw
Animal rennet
Affinage of 3 months
Available year-round
Farmstead
Similar to Baby Swiss

This producer's herd is almost entirely composed of Milking Shorthorns because of their temperament in the milking parlor and ability to withstand the rigors of heat and cold in southern Washington. The animals spend as much time on pasture as possible, coming into the barn only during heavy rains, as required by state law. These small wheels have a semi-firm texture and golden straw color, similar to a mild, Baby Swiss.

NAUGHTY NELLIE

River Valley Cheese • Fall City, WA

Amber ale

Brown Swiss

Washed rind
2 lb., 4 lb., 8 lb., or 10 lb. wheel
Raw
Microbial coagulant
Affinage of 70 days
Available year-round
Farmstead
Similar to Port-Salut

Naughty Nellie wheels are named for the golden Pike Brewery ale that they are bathed in throughout their aging. This farmstead producer milks just a handful of Brown Swiss cows, which are out on pasture whenever weather permits and fed spent brewers grain from nearby Pike Place Brewery. The paste of these pudgy wheels is springy on the tongue with hints of malt on the finish.

NOCCIOLA

Tumalo Farms • Bend, OR

Brown ale

Saanen and French Alpine

Semi-firm
9 lb. wheel
Pasteurized
Animal rennet
Affinage of 3 months
Available year-round
Farmstead
Similar to goat Gouda

This cheese pays its respects to the hazelnut (or nocciola in Italian), a large crop in Oregon. The curds are washed and cooked before the nuts are scattered throughout. Once the two are thoroughly mixed together they are scooped into forms to be pressed. After the cheeses are popped out of their forms they begin the three to six month aging process. The paste is semi-firm and tastes of light caramel. The hazelnuts add their own subtle sweetness and toothsome texture.

NOCTURNE

Andante Dairy • Petaluma, CA

Chenin blanc

Jersey

Bloomy rind
6–8 oz. truncated pyramid
Pasteurized
Microbial coagulant
Affinage of 2 weeks
Available year-round
Creamery
Similar to Valençay

The rind of this soft-ripened, truncated pyramid appears almost gray because of the layer of vegetable ash sprinkled on the cheese after draining and unhooping. Dusty white molds develop on the surface as the cheese matures, obscuring the black ash. Directly beneath the rind, the paste breaks down into a silky texture while the interior resembles a moist, dense cake.

NORTHERN GOLD

Pedrozo Dairy and Cheese Company • Orland, CA

Chardonnay

Holstein and Jersey

Semi-firm
8–10 lb. wheel
Raw
Microbial coagulant
Affinage of 2 months
Available year-round
Farmstead
Similar to young fontina

This raw, farmstead tomme is made with milk from a herd of twenty-five Holstein and Jersey cows that are kept in a pasture-based system. The Pedrozo's learned how to make Northern Gold from the farm's previous owners. Wheels range from eight to ten pounds and have a pudgy, semi-soft texture, and a natural, golden rind. Vegetal flavors of damp hay develop gradually over the two-month affinage.

N. W. COMFORT

Blue Rose Dairy • Winlock, WA

Prosecco

Primarily Saanen

Semi-soft
4–5 lb. wheel
Raw
Animal rennet
Affinage of 2 months
Available year-round
Farmstead
Similar to ricotta salata

These interesting wheels are considered a natural rind cheese but they actually remain a creamy white color instead of developing the typical dusty gray and brown molds. The cheese is rubbed with olive oil throughout its development, which keeps the rind moist and prevents cracking, and also discourages any mold growth. The paste smells like cream cheese at the center and like a damp cellar toward the rind. The flavors follow suit: acidic, almost sharp, at the center and woodsy next to the rind.

OAXACA

Sometimes referred to as Mexican mozzarella, Oaxaca is part of the pasta filata cheese family. The production involves submerging the curds in extremely hot water and then stretching and pulling them into long ribbons. Oaxaca's flavor is similar to that of mozzarella—fresh and milky with a hint of salt. It can be made from either cow or goat milk. A simple way to make Oaxaca even more refreshing is to douse it with lime juice and add a dash of salt.

El Michoacano
Animal rennet • Creamery

Ochoa Cheese Factory
Animal rennet • Creamery

OLD APPLETREE TOMME

Estrella Family Creamery • Montesano, WA

Muscat

Primarily Normandy

Semi-firm
4.5 lb. wheel
Raw
Animal rennet
Affinage of 2 months
Available year-round
Farmstead
Similar to Gruyère

The bright yellow paste of Old Appletree Tomme (a result of the herd grazing on lush pasture for much of the year) is a splendid contrast with the dusty, peach hue of the rind. The wide, low wheels are washed in cider and apple brandy throughout their two to three months of aging. The cheese is springy and a little bit bendy but breaks down into a nice lactic paste on the tongue. The flavor is reminiscent of a young, nutty, salty, slightly pungent Gruyère.

The Estrellas also produce Vineyard Tomme, a seasonal specialty made by burying Old Appletree Tommes in grape must from local wineries. Occasionally this cheese is available in time for Thanksgiving but it all depends on the timing of the grape harvest.

OLD WORLD PORTUGUESE

Spring Hill Cheese Company • Petaluma, CA

Chardonnay

Jersey

Hard
8 lb. square
Pasteurized
Microbial coagulant
Affinage of 6 months
Available year-round
Creamery
Certified Organic
Similar to Sao Jorge

This cheese is modeled on the famous Portuguese cheese, Sao Jorge, that Joe Matos (of Matos Cheese Factory) introduced to Sonoma County in the 1970s. The texture of Old World Portuguese is a bit waxy and craggy, crumbling a bit when cut. The paste tastes of reduced fresh butter with an occasional grassy bite and a slight hint of coconut on the finish.

OPAL CREEK

Ancient Heritage Dairy • Scio, OR

IPA

Ayrshire and Guernsey

East Friesian and Lacaune

Washed rind
5 lb. wheel
Raw
Animal rennet
Affinage of 3 months
Available year-round
Farmstead
Similar to Gubbeen

Washed rind cheeses can be divided into two classes: those described as pungent and others that are more aptly described as meaty. This cheese falls into the latter category with a combination of bright lactic flavors and savory beefy notes. A meal within a cheese! The rind is a vibrant shade of orange, a wonderful contrast to the slightly yellow tone of the paste. The texture is moist and the paste is tacky to the touch but becomes creamy on the tongue. Depending on the time of year, Opal Creek can be made with a combination of cow and sheep milk, or (when the sheep are dried off) only cow milk.

OREGON BLUE

Rogue Creamery • Central Point, OR

Maury

Brown Swiss, Holstein, and Brown Swiss–Holstein cross

Blue
5 lb. wheel
Raw
Microbial coagulant
Affinage of 6 months
Available year-round
Creamery
Food Alliance Sustainable Producer
Similar to Roquefort

This cheese has a great history as the first blue cheese produced in the western United States. The founder of Rogue Creamery, Tom Vella, was inspired to make a blue cheese after visiting the Roquefort caves in France back in 1957. Though Oregon Blue is made with cow milk, instead of the sheep milk traditionally used for Roquefort, the development of the blue molds and the method of production yield a cheese that is similar in its dusty, blue flavor and creamy, butter-like texture. Wheels of Oregon Blue are dry salted, pierced, and then dipped in wax to prevent the growth of any rind. Once their maturation is complete, the wax is peeled off and they are wrapped in foil.

OREGONZOLA

Rogue Creamery • Central Point, OR

Stout

Brown Swiss, Holstein, and Brown Swiss–Holstein cross

Blue
5 lb. wheel
Raw
Microbial coagulant
Affinage of 4 months
Available year-round
Creamery
Food Alliance Sustainable Producer
Similar to Gorgonzola

Modeled on Italy's famous Gorgonzola blue cheese, Oregonzola has brilliant winey flavors and a small bite on the finish. The thick texture verges on fudgy and is scattered throughout with tyrosine crystals. Most wheels are released at the age of four months though some are held in reserve up to eight months.

OTENTIQUE

Juniper Grove Farm • Redmond, OR

Grenache

Mixed herd

Surface-ripened
5 oz. disk
Raw
Microbial coagulant
Affinage of 2 months
Available year-round
Farmstead
Similar to Pélardon

It's evident that Pierre Kolisch was inspired by the cheeses he experienced during the time he spent travelling in France in preparation for starting his farmstead operation. Otentique, a small, raw milk, surface-ripened disk, has a savory depth of flavor at its center and a dense, clay-like texture. The broken down paste beneath the slightly piquant rind has funky vegetal notes similar to the smell of barnyard and wet hay.

PANEER

Cowgirl Creamery • Petaluma, CA

Riesling

Holstein, Jersey, and Holstein–Jersey cross

Fresh
8 oz. tub
Pasteurized
Microbial coagulant
No affinage
Available year-round
Creamery
Certified Organic
Similar to triple cream fromage blanc

Paneer cheese is most often associated with Asia, where the exact methods of production and resulting cheeses vary from region to region. The basic recipe for paneer cheese is simple, in fact, the production is quite similar to that of whole milk ricotta: milk is acidified with lemon juice or vinegar, heated until the milk solids loosely knit together, and then scooped out into cloth or forms to drain. The paneer familiar to most of us is pressed into a rectangular form, and then cubed and added to a variety of savory or sweet dishes.

Cowgirl Creamery's Paneer is quite different because it is not pressed and cream is added during its production. Consequently, the cheese is much higher in moisture than traditional paneer and thus creamier and spreadable. It is also made with a bit of microbial coagulant that keeps the cheese from becoming tart or acidic.

PANELA

El Michoacano • Marysville, WA

Amber ale

Jersey

Fresh
Size and shape varies
Pasteurized
Animal rennet
No affinage
Available year-round
Creamery
Similar to Asadero or queso blanco

Similar to queso blanco, Panela does not melt easily even though it has a relatively high moisture content. The texture is almost like firm tofu but with more moisture. The rindless paste tastes of milk bordering on custard. A touch of salt brings out the natural sweet flavors of the rich Jersey milk. Panela is perfect for torta-style sandwiches or a simple snack.

PARMESAN

Lambrusco

The great Italian cheese Parmigiano-Reggiano is a protected cheese; in order for a cheese to bear that name it must be produced within a specific region of Italy and according to designated methods. In the United States, any cheeses made in the style of Parmigiano-Reggiano must have some other name and often the name used is Parmesan.

Parmesan cheese often has a hard paste and caramel, salty, and piquant flavors. Most wheels will have some kind of natural rind.

Golden Glen Creamery
2 lb. or 13 lb. wheel • Pasteurized • Microbial coagulant • Affinage of 6 months • Farmstead

Gothberg Farms
4–6 lb. wheel • Raw • Animal rennet • Affinage of 9 months • Farmstead

Pine Stump Farms
3 lb. wheel • Raw • Microbial coagulant • Affinage of 6 months • Farmstead

Craft Spotlight: Estrella Family Creamery

Kelli Estrella had been a hobbyist cheesemaker for more than fifteen years when she began selling cheese from her licensed creamery in 2003. Her passion for cheesemaking comes through in every piece and wheel that leaves the Estrella's farmstead operation. Kelli and her husband, Anthony, had dreamed of moving to the country for years. Eventually, in 2001, they bought a 164-acre farm with plans to bring the defunct dairy property back to life. The farm is located in a traditional dairying region of Washington, southwest of Seattle and about fifteen miles inland from the coastal town of Aberdeen. This area is known for rich soil that produces lush pastures.

The couple and their children built up healthy, pastured herds of Normandy cows and LaMancha goats; these herds produce all the milk for Estrella Family Creamery's eighteen varieties of cheese. Kelli often gives credit for her cheeses to the high-quality milk that their animals produce but the Estrellas deserve some of the credit too. They have committed to a lifestyle that involves making cheese twice daily, every twelve hours, so that the milk from their animals never goes into a bulk tank to be cooled and held over until it is time for cheesemaking. Every time the animals are milked that milk is immediately turned into cheese.

In 2007, the Estrellas built an in-ground aging room in a hillside near the cheese room. The cellar does not require refrigeration because it is buried underground. Working with the aging room was a learning experience for them as it took time to understand how to maintain the ideal temperature and humidity for all the varieties of cheese that they make.

The range of cheeses produced by the Estrellas is staggering: Cheddar, tomme, blue, bloomy, and even washed rinds. All cheeses are made with raw milk and thus are aged a minimum of sixty days to fulfill FDA requirements. Properly caring for such a wide variety of cheese types for that length of time requires an enormous amount of work. Kelli has the benefit of an abundant supply of high-quality cow and goat milk but it is her skilled hands that turn out wheels and drums that can showcase the abundance of flavor that milk contains.

PARTLY SUNNY

Estrella Family Creamery • Montesano, WA

Moscato d'Asti

Primarily Normandy

Blue
1 lb. drum
Raw
Animal rennet
Affinage of 2 months
Available year-round
Farmstead
Similar to Rocbleu

Defined by its place of origin, Partly Sunny was named in honor of the weatherman's near daily forecast for Montesano, Washington. These drum-shaped blue wheels are pierced, to allow the blue veins to grow throughout the paste, and then encouraged to develop a light bloom on their rinds. The blue mold used in this recipe has dusty and leathery flavors that nicely compliment the notes of dry hay that come through in the milk. The texture is rich, like clay.

PAVE

Pug's Leap Farm • Healdsburg, CA

Champagne

Mixed herd

Surface-ripened
6–8 oz. truncated pyramid
Pasteurized
Animal rennet
Affinage of 3 weeks
Available late spring through early winter
Farmstead
Similar to Pouligny-Saint-Pierre

The goat milk for this truncated pyramid comes from the small farmstead at Pug's Leap, nestled in the midst of Sonoma's wine country. Pave has a sturdy, wrinkly, white rind, and a clay-like texture that melts on the tongue. Funky, vegetal flavors are backed up by vibrant, briney, and tangy notes characteristic of young goat milk cheeses.

PEARL

Ancient Heritage Dairy • Scio, OR

Viognier

Ayrshire and Guernsey

Surface-ripened
3–4 oz. disk
Pasteurized
Animal rennet
Affinage of 3 weeks
Available year-round
Farmstead
Similar to St. Felicien

This small cheese is surface-ripened with a variety of molds, including *Penicilium candidum* which is known for making bloomy rinds *bloom*. Ancient Heritage Dairy's six milking cows are mostly Ayrshires but they've mixed in Guernseys to boost the fat content, guaranteeing a luscious and creamy cheese. Making Pearl is a long process: the cultures and milk are mixed and allowed to rest together for thirty hours before a touch of rennet is added, the curd is cut, and the cheeses are formed. A light dusting of ash on the surface of the cheese creates a dark backdrop for the mottled white rind. Some of the disks take up to five weeks to ripen.

PECORINO

Black Sheep Creamery • Adna, WA

Chianti

East Friesian and Rideau Arcott

Hard
4.5–5 lb. or 9 lb. wheel
Raw
Microbial coagulant
Affinage of 6 months
Available late fall through early winter
Farmstead
Similar to aged pecorino

A rare and special treat, the Pecorino made by Black Sheep Creamery is only available in November, December, and January, and in very small quantities. These are the longest aged wheels produced by the creamery. They are brined after coming out of their forms, and then rubbed repeatedly throughout their development with olive oil to keep the rind from developing cracks and to prevent the growth of surface molds.

PEPATO

Bellwether Farms • Petaluma, CA

Nero d'Avola

East Friesian and Lacaune

Semi-firm
4 lb. wheel
Raw
Animal rennet
Affinage of 3 months
Available year-round
Creamery
Similar to Italian Pepato

Studded with rugged, whole black peppercorns, these wheels develop aromas of wine and spice. Made in a style similar to Bellwether Farms' San Andreas, the wheels of Pepato exhibit the classic flavors of nuts and grains typical in modestly aged Pecorinos. The robust bite of peppercorns makes Pepato an interesting addition to a cheese plate or shaved over pasta dishes.

PERRYDALE

Willamette Valley Cheese Company • Salem, OR

Brown ale

Jersey

Mixed herd

Semi-soft
10 lb. wheel
Pasteurized
Microbial coagulant
Affinage of 1 year
Available spring through summer
Farmstead and Creamery
Similar to young Ossau-Iraty

These mixed milk wheels are often in short supply because the milking cycle for sheep is so brief. The sheep milk, bought from a farmer who milks his sheep herd seasonally from late April through early September, is mixed with cow milk from Willamette Valley Cheese Company's herd of Jerseys. The wheels develop a natural rind over the course of their year-long aging. The surprisingly pliable paste has tangy flavors crossed with caramel notes.

PETIT BONHEUR

Rivers Edge Chèvre • Logsden, OR

Cava

Alpine

Bloomy rind
6–7 oz. heart
Pasteurized
Animal rennet
Affinage of 15 days
Available year-round
Farmstead
Similar to Coeur de Berry

Hearts are a lovely, whimsical shape for goat cheese and Rivers Edge Chèvre makes two different versions. The milk for each comes exclusively from their modest herd of less than sixty goats, which are out on pasture whenever weather and their mood permits. The cheeses are made from fresh goat curds that are scooped into heart-shaped molds. Petit Bonheur is sprinkled with paprika after it comes out of its form. The curds for Heart's Desire are mixed with pink peppercorns prior to going into their forms. Both are encouraged to develop a bloomy rind over their surface and within two weeks the paste beneath the rind begins to soften. Eventually the paste will fully break down, turning even the velvety center into a gooey liquid.

PETIT MARCEL

Pug's Leap Farm • Healdsburg, CA

Côtes du Rhône

Mixed herd

Surface-ripened
3–4 oz. disk
Pasteurized
Animal rennet
Affinage of 10–14 days
Available late spring through early winter
Farmstead
Similar to Picodon

Petit Marcel is shaped like a bulky, oversized coin. The paste is dense but not dry in texture and becomes creamy on the palate. The flavors of the paste are bright and lactic, like sour cream, and combine pleasantly with the slightly earthy flavors of the thin rind.

PIANOFORTE

Andante Dairy • Petaluma, CA

Sweet Vouvray

Jersey

Bloomy rind
5–6 oz. disk
Pasteurized
Microbial coagulant
Affinage of 3 weeks
Available year-round
Creamery
Similar to Saint-Marcellin

The cheesemaker at Andante Dairy describes Pianoforte as having a soft texture and a loud flavor. This cow's milk cheese is shaped like a disk and covered with a wrinkly rind. As the paste softens, breaking down almost to a liquid, the flavors of fresh milk and mulch become bolder.

PIERCE POINT

Cowgirl Creamery • Petaluma, CA

Old world pinot noir

Holstein, Jersey, and Holstein–Jersey cross

Bloomy rind
10 oz. drum
Pasteurized
Microbial coagulant
Affinage of 1 month
Available fall through winter
Creamery
Certified Organic
Similar to Fleur du Maquis

Only made in the fall and winter when the fat content of the cow milk is high, this cheese is dedicated to showcasing the bounty of the region. The small wheels are washed in muscato wine and rolled in organic, dried herbs that grow naturally in the Tomales Bay area of California's coast. A light, bloomy rind is encouraged to develop over the herb coating (a mixture of fennel seed, coriander, marigold, red clover, and chamomile). The herbs add a savory depth to the buttery flavor of the paste, which ranges from crumbly at the interior to smooth and fudgy beneath the rind.

PINE STUMP FARMS ASIAGO

Pine Stump Farms • Omak, WA

Sangiovese

Mixed herd

Hard
3 lb. wheel
Raw
Microbial coagulant
Affinage of 6 months
Available year-round
Farmstead
Similar to Ibores

The high-steppe terrain of Pine Stump Farms does not sustain enough growth to graze the goats on pasture year-round. Aside from fresh spring grasses, the goats' feed primarily comes from high-quality, organic alfalfa hay produced during growing season on the farm. Asiago is a hard cheese so the curds are pressed in their forms and then brined before going into the cooler for aging. It's tough to maintain humidity in the climate of eastern Washington (especially when aging more than sixty days) so the wheels are dipped in wax to protect them from the dry environment.

PLEASANT VALLEY

Pholia Farm • Rogue River, OR

Alsatian riesling

Nigerian Dwarf

Semi-firm
9 lb. wheel
Raw
Microbial coagulant
Affinage of 6 months
Available winter through early spring
Farmstead
Similar to Gruyère

Pholia Farm uses Nigerian Dwarf goats, a smaller breed than other dairy goats, which produce milk loaded with protein and fat. The components and yields of Nigerian Dwarf milk are actually closer to that of dairy sheep than to regular goat milk. This milk works incredibly well for Pleasant Valley, a mountain-style cheese that is cooked, pressed, and aged for a minimum of six months. Because of the higher levels of protein and fat, the paste is firm and closed, yet creamy on the tongue. The flavors that unfold make up a complex, savory, vegetal bouquet that is reminiscent of the finest Gruyères.

Sustainability Spotlight: Pholia Farm

Gianaclis and Vern Caldwell purchased their first dairy goats because Gianaclis wanted to have fresh milk for her family like she had while growing up. They bought a unique goat breed called Nigerian Dwarf whose defining characteristics are their small size (they stand two feet tall when fully grown) and the high protein and fat components of their milk. At the time, size was the most important feature because the Caldwell's youngest daughter, Amelia, was eight years old and could easily handle the small goats.

When Vern retired from the Marine Corps the family moved back to a parcel of the property where Gianaclis was raised in southern Oregon. While they were experimenting in their kitchen, making cheese and soap with their goat milk, they were also busy building an off-the-grid dairy farm and residence. Power is supplied to the dairy and their home by solar panels and a micro-hydro turbine run by a small, seasonal creek on the property. In the dairy and cheese room, which need a lot of hot water for cleaning, they installed a high-efficiency, low emissions, indoor wood boiler. A visit to Pholia Farm will have you reconsidering any notions that living off-the-grid means compromising quality of life.

The Caldwells have been able to keep the size of their herd to just under twenty goats by creating other sources of revenue for the farm, such as animal husbandry and cheesemaking classes for aspiring producers. And given the small community of Nigerian Dwarf owners, with a bit of effort, Pholia has become a source of solid breeding stock. The evolution of Pholia Farm is an inspiration: not only have the Caldwells expertly executed their vision for a sustainable farm but they have created a lifestyle and a livelihood that suits them completely.

POINT REYES ORIGINAL BLUE

Point Reyes Farmstead Cheese Company • Point Reyes Station, CA

Riesling

Holstein

Blue
3 lb. or 6 lb. wheel
Raw
Microbial coagulant
Affinage of 6 months
Available year-round
Farmstead
Similar to Maytag Blue

Since emerging on the market in 2000 this blue cheese has become a California classic. All of the milk comes from the herd of Holsteins on the Giacomini family's dairy farm, situated on a small inlet on northern California's coastline. Milk coming into the cheese room is separated: skim goes straight into the vat and cream is homogenized before being added back into the vats. This treatment improves the texture of the cheese for developing blue mold in the wheels, and also adds a creamier texture to the finished cheese. Once the wheels come out of their forms, they are cured for three weeks at a specific temperature and humidity during which time they are hand-salted, flipped, and eventually pierced with needles to allow oxygen to activate the blue mold. Point Reyes Original Blue has contrasting flavors of fresh milk and piquant blue mold, making it a fantastic cheese on its own, served with pecans and a dollop of honey, or crumbled atop a salad.

PONDHOPPER

Tumalo Farms • Bend, OR

Pale ale

Saanen and French Alpine

Semi-soft
9–10 lb. wheel
Pasteurized
Animal rennet
Affinage of 2 months
Available year-round
Farmstead
Similar to goat Gouda

The name of this cheese is a reference to the hops in the local microbrew that the producer adds to the milk during cheesemaking. The curds are washed, cooked, and then pressed, and as a result the paste is thick and creamy. The agreeable acidity up front is followed by mellow flavors of toffee and hops.

PORT EDISON

Samish Bay Cheese Company • Bow, WA

Hard cider

Jersey, Milking Shorthorn, and Jersey–Milking Shorthorn cross

Semi-firm
1 lb., 2 lb., or 6–8 lb. wheel
Raw
Microbial coagulant
Affinage of 6 months
Available year-round
Farmstead
Certified Organic
Similar to sharp Cheddar

Port Edison is a more recent creation than the other aged cheeses at Samish Bay; the oldest wheels around the cellar have about six to seven years of age on them. These wheels are slightly higher in moisture making the texture a bit more supple. The paste has a lively, sharp bite.

POZO TOMME

Rinconada Dairy • Santa Margarita, CA

Chianti

East Friesian–Lacaune cross

Hard
5–6 lb. wheel
Raw
Animal rennet
Affinage of 2 months
Available late spring through fall
Farmstead
Similar to pecorino

This farmstead creamery lets their herd of East Friesian and Lacaune ewes out on pasture whenever weather permits. Milking season is brief (May through July) meaning that cheeses are not generally available year-round. These wheels, aged a minimum of two months, are reminiscent in texture and flavor of Italy's best aged pecorinos. Firm and dry in appearance, the paste softens up on the palate. The sharp finish makes this cheese an appealing grating cheese. Pozo Tomme is also nice as a table cheese accompanied by toasted hazelnuts and lighter honey such as star thistle or lavender.

PYRAMID

Juniper Grove Farm • Redmond, OR

Dry riesling

Mixed herd

Surface-ripened
6.5 oz. pyramid
Raw
Microbial coagulant
Affinage of 2 months
Available year-round
Farmstead
Similar to Pouligny-Saint-Pierre

The pyramid is a challenging shape for cheese as it does not lend itself to obvious flipping and turning during the aging process. Juniper Grove's Pyramid is made from raw goat milk and thus must age for a minimum of two months. The large surface area requires that the mold and yeast activity on the rind be appropriately paced or the interior will break down too quickly and compromise the cheese's structure. The cakey interior which is surrounded by creamy paste and encapsulated in a crinkled skin is proof that cheesemaker Pierre Kolisch has mastered the art of slow ripening. As the cheese ages and loses moisture, the paste tightens and flavors become robust and barnyardy.

QUARK

This fresh cheese is made from pasteurized milk, sometimes with added cream. The coagulation is entirely lactic; nothing beyond the starter culture is used to coagulate the solids to form curds. The resulting cheese is drier in texture than cream cheese and has a tangy flavor. Quark is often used in baking similar to the way one would use ricotta. It can also replace cream cheese on sandwiches and bagels or be served as an accompaniment to fresh fruit.

Appel Farms Farmstead

Marin French Cheese Company Creamery

Spring Hill Cheese Company Creamery

QUESO DE OVEJA

Black Sheep Creamery • Adna, WA

Hefeweizen

East Friesian and Rideau Arcott

Hard
3.5–4.25 lb. wheel
Raw
Microbial coagulant
Affinage of 3 months
Available summer through fall
Farmstead
Similar to Idiazabal

Although the producer uses the same basic recipe to make Black Sheep and Tin Willow Tommes, different starter and secondary cultures create a unique flavor profile for Queso de Oveja. The cheese's toothsome texture is dry but not crumbly and maintains a gentle roux-like grittiness. The paste has a rustic meaty quality, toasted notes, and a hint of lemony acidity that balances out the richness. Wheels are brined when they come out of their forms to prevent unwanted molds from developing on the natural, dusty beige rind.

QUESO FRESCO

While the production of this cheese is not standardized anywhere in the world, the name queso fresco usually indicates a fresh cheese that has a crumbly texture, a mild lactic flavor, and a touch of saltiness. Queso fresco is great crumbled over beans and salads or as a stuffing for peppers and other vegetables.

Bodega Goat Cheese Farmstead

El Michoacano Creamery

Ochoa Cheese Factory Creamery

Queseria Bendita Creamery

Samish Bay Cheese Company Farmstead

RED DARLA

Estrella Family Creamery • Montesano, WA

Gamay

Primarily Normandy

Washed rind
I lb. wheel
Raw
Animal rennet
Affinage of 2 months
Available year-round
Farmstead
Similar to Aisy Cendré

Many Estrella Family Creamery cheeses are named after their animals and Red Darla is no exception. The Estrellas use the same recipe as for their Dominoes cheese, which is named after Darla's bovine mother—the only difference is that the wheels of Red Darla are washed in red wine throughout their aging. The result of this washing is the development of a sticky, stinky rind, and beefy, more pungent flavors in the paste. These pudgy little wheels are both tacky and creamy at once.

RED HAWK

Cowgirl Creamery • Petaluma, CA

Sauternes

Holstein, Jersey, and Holstein–Jersey cross

Washed rind
12 oz. drum
Pasteurized
Microbial coagulant
Affinage of 5 weeks
Available year-round
Creamery
Certified Organic
Similar to Limburger crossed with Saint André

The creation of this cheese was more of a discovery than a plan. When one batch of Mt. Tam, another triple cream cheese produced by Cowgirl Creamery, developed some undesirable molds on their surfaces the cheesemakers washed them with brine in an attempt to solve the problem. This extra treatment created the ideal environment for *Brevibacterium linens*, the bacteria responsible for pungent aromas and flavors in the orange-hued cheeses we call washed rinds. Dense fog and ocean air are desirable conditions for the development of *B. linens* so the creamery's location along the California coast turned out to be an ideal fit. The producers could not call this cheese Mt. Tam so they gave it a new name and promptly sold out of Red Hawk at the local farmers' markets.

REDMONDO

Juniper Grove Farm • Redmond, OR

Oloroso sherry

Mixed herd

Hard
4 lb. wheel
Raw
Microbial coagulant
Affinage of 9 months
Available year-round
Farmstead
Similar to aged pecorino

The recipe for these wheels, based on the production of aged Italian pecorinos, involves curds that have been cooked and stirred. Aged for a minimum of nine months, the texture is dense and firm. The paste tastes of toasted almonds and smells like dulce de leche. Cheesemaker and owner Pierre Kolisch also makes a younger version of this cheese, aged a mere two months, that he calls Farmer's Cheese. The young wheels aren't allowed to develop much of a rind and have a closed, bendy texture and touch of milky sweetness.

REDWOOD LOG

Shamrock Artisan Goat Cheese • Willits, CA

Chenin blanc

Purebred Alpine, Nubian, and LaMancha

Semi-firm
6–8 oz. log
Pasteurized
Microbial coagulant
Affinage of 3 months
Available year-round
Farmstead
Similar to Pierre Dorée

This farmstead producer boasts the distinction of having a closed herd meaning that all of their animals are birthed from does within their herd. The mixture of goat breeds (purebred Alpine, Nubian, and LaMancha) provides a workable combination of good temperament, components, and decent milk volume. Redwood Log is a small goat milk stick that is not allowed to develop much of a rind and is aged for a minimum of three months. This relatively long affinage gives it a firm texture and a sharper flavor than similarly shaped cheeses that are much younger and have higher moisture content. Shamrock Bouchon is the smaller (three- to five-ounce) version of this cheese. Both sizes work well as grating cheeses because of their firm texture and peppery flavors.

RENATA

Sally Jackson Cheeses • Oroville, WA

Vin jaune

Brown Swiss

Semi-soft
2 lb. wheel
Raw
Animal rennet
Affinage of 2 months
Available late spring through early winter
Farmstead
Similar to Reblochon

The name for this cheese comes from one of Sally Jackson's two milking cows. The curds are scooped into molds and left to drain through gravity rather than being pressed. Each wheel is allowed to develop a bit of a natural rind, molds and all, before being wrapped in chestnut leaves to finish aging. The rind aids in the breakdown of the paste until it becomes pudgy and luscious in texture. Winey, fermented notes are balanced by a combination of lactic and barnyard flavors.

RICOTTA

Traditionally, ricotta was simply a by-product of cheesemaking. During the making and draining of hard cheeses, not all of the solids in milk get collected into curds. Making ricotta was a way to gather up all the proteins and fats that remained in the whey. After the reserved whey was heated, any solids that floated to the surface were collected and put into forms to drain. It could either be consumed as a slightly sweet tasting fresh cheese or aged out to develop sharper flavors.

Today, ricotta is mostly made by adding a mild acidifying agent such as vinegar, lemon juice, or a starter culture, to warm whole milk. The milk is heated until the solids begin to clump together and can be scooped out into forms. The flavor and texture of whole milk ricotta varies greatly from producer to producer because so much depends on the fat and protein content of the milk and the amount of acidification. In general, whole milk ricotta tends to be a bit creamier than traditional ricotta.

Requesón is a Mexican-style ricotta which can be made using a variety of methods such as reheating whey, acidifying whole milk, and sometimes adding cream too. Made in Spain and throughout the Americas, requesón varies between regions from a cheese similar in texture and flavor to ricotta to something that resembles flan because of its silken, almost custardy flavor.

Ricotta and requesón are often used in cooking but can also serve as refreshingly simple table cheeses with fresh herbs mixed in or honey drizzled over the top.

Belfiore Cheese Company
Whole milk ricotta
Creamery

Bellwether Farms
Whole milk ricotta
Creamery

Bellwether Farms
Traditional ricotta
Creamery

Black Sheep Creamery
Traditional ricotta
Farmstead

Bodega Artisan Cheese
Whole milk ricotta
Farmstead

El Michoacano
Whole milk requesón
Creamery

Gioia Cheese Company
Whole milk ricotta
Creamery

Gothberg Farms
Whole milk ricotta
Farmstead

Harley Farms
Whole milk ricotta
Farmstead

Jacobs Creamery
Whole milk ricotta
Creamery

Queseria Bendita
Whole milk requesón
Creamery

River Valley Cheese
Whole milk ricotta
Farmstead

RIO SANTIAM

Fraga Farm • Sweet Home, OR

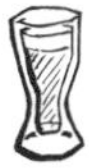

Red ale

Alpine, Nubian,
and Alpine–Nubian cross

Semi-firm
3 lb. wheel
Raw
Microbial coagulant
Affinage of 2 months
Available year-round
Farmstead
Certified Organic
Similar to Mahon

The orange-pink coloring of the rinds is a result of infrequent washing throughout the development of these wheels. The semi-firm paste can become somewhat dry in wheels aged out beyond six months. Aromas of apricot and earth permeate the rind, and prominent tangy and salty flavors give way to a nutty finish.

ROGUE RIVER BLUE

Rogue Creamery • Central Point, OR

Tojkai

Brown Swiss, Holstein, and Brown Swiss–Holstein cross

Blue
5 lb. wheel
Raw
Microbial coagulant
Affinage of 10 months
Available late summer through fall
Creamery
Food Alliance Sustainable Producer
Similar to Valdeón

This blue cheese was designed to showcase the seasonal shifts in the milk used by Rogue Creamery and the agricultural bounty of Oregon. Wheels of Rogue River Blue are made only from the autumnal equinox through the end of pasture-based feeding. The base recipe is the same one used to make Oregon Blue but the milk has a higher butterfat content during the fall. Each wheel is wrapped in eight grape leaves that have been macerated in Pear Brandy from Portland's Clear Creek Distillery. Once wheels have been wrapped and sealed, they are aged for at least ten months, if not a full year, before being released to the public. The paste has a complex bouquet that includes tart, red fruit notes, and robust, heady flavors of butter and bacon. The texture is moist and luscious from months of aging in their wrappings.

ROMANELLO

Vella Cheese Company • Sonoma, CA

Bourbon

Holstein and Guernsey

Semi-firm
10 lb. wheel
Raw
Microbial coagulant
Affinage of 6–7 months
Available year-round
Creamery
Similar to young Romano

Romanello is a newer development from Ignazio Vella, the master cheesemaker at Vella Cheese Company. Designed to mimic a young Romano cheese (a Romano without the sharpness that comes from aging), these wheels have butterscotch flavors and a satisfying bite on the finish. The texture becomes hard and craggy over the six-month aging period but remains fudgy on the palate. Romanello works as a table cheese and would also be a nice grating cheese.

ROSA

Ancient Heritage Dairy • Scio, WA

Nebbiolo

Ayrshire and Guernsey

East Friesian–Lacaune cross

Hard
9 lb. wheel
Raw
Animal rennet
Affinage of 5 months
Available summer through fall
Farmstead
Similar to young fontina crossed with provolone

Ancient Heritage Dairy sometimes blends cow milk in with the sheep milk in order to make more wheels of Rosa. With an affinage of five months, the paste of this cheese becomes firmer but maintains a creamy consistency similar to Italian mountain cheeses like fontina. The secondary cultures add a pungent nearly sour bite to the finish.

ROSA RUGOSA

Larkhaven Farmstead Cheese • Tonasket, WA

Brown ale

Mixed herd

East Friesian crossed with several breeds

Semi-firm
2–3 lb. wheel
Raw
Animal rennet
Affinage of 2 months
Available summer through winter
Farmstead
Similar to Corsican goat tomme

This tomme's namesake, a wild, European rose, seems absolutely appropriate given the rustic appearance and flavors of this mixed milk cheese. The blend of goat and sheep milk present earthy, herbaceous flavors with a citrusy note of acidity. The wheels are washed throughout the aging process, coloring the rinds a bright combination of orange and pink, and adding a slightly pungent background to the sliceable yet crumbly, semi-firm paste.

ROUGE ET NOIR BREAKFAST CHEESE

Marin French Cheese Company • Petaluma, CA

Champagne

Jersey and Guernsey

Fresh
3 oz. disk
Pasteurized
Microbial coagulant
No affinage
Available year-round
Creamery
Similar to fromage frais

This small disk of fresh, cow milk cheese has a lemony flavor. The use of Jersey and Guernsey milk from local dairies shows in the golden yellow color of the paste. The texture is light but not quite spreadable. Though it does not have a rind, the exterior is drier than the moist paste; if left longer than three weeks, it will begin to grow a delicate bloomy rind because the recipe uses a Brie culture.

ROUGE ET NOIR BRIE

Marin French Cheese Company • Petaluma, CA

Champagne

Jersey and Guernsey

Bloomy rind
8 oz. and 16 oz. disk
Pasteurized
Microbial coagulant
Affinage of 2 weeks
Available year-round
Creamery
Similar to Brie

One unique feature of the Rouge et Noir Brie is its melty, buttery texture (the paste nearly dissolves on the tongue) distinguishing it from traditional Brie which has a tacky, globby texture. The paste of Rouge et Noir Brie is a brilliant shade of yellow because it is made with milk from Jersey cows. Jerseys absorb more beta-carotene from the grass and forage they eat and the natural pigment of that beta-carotene colors the milk.

ROUGE ET NOIR MARIN FRENCH GOLD

Marin French Cheese Company • Petaluma, CA

German pinot gris

Jersey and Guernsey

Bloomy rind
24 oz. disk
Pasteurized
Microbial coagulant
Affinage of 2 weeks
Available year-round
Creamery
Similar to Brie

This bloomy-coated cheese is a triple cream version of a traditional Brie recipe. This means that the butterfat content is at least 75 percent, the texture is a touch creamier, and the flavors are closer to butter than fresh milk. When young, the center of Rouge et Noir Marin French Gold can verge on crumbly because it has yet to break down into a smooth paste.

Marin French makes a blue version of this goat milk Camembert, Rouge et Noir Marin Chevre Blue, in which the subtle, cooked goat milk sweetness is offset by musty flavored blue veins. The dusty blue flavors blend nicely with the notes of fresh butter and hay.

ROUGE ET NOIR SCHLOSSKRANZ

Marin French Cheese Company • Petaluma, CA

Porter

Jersey and Guernsey

Washed rind
2 lb. wreath
Pasteurized
Microbial coagulant
Affinage of 3 weeks
Available year-round
Creamery
Similar to Liederkranz

Schlosskranz directly translates to the castle wreath, describing the shape of this washed rind cheese. The texture of the paste is smooth and the rind is slightly toothsome. The paste's pungency and flavors of bittersweet chocolate are balanced out by underlying notes of fresh milk. Smear this cheese on some pumpernickel bread and enjoy with a rich dark beer. Marin French Cheese Company sells the center of the wreath, Schlosskranz-Herz, as well as Schloss, a six-ounce brick-shaped version of Schlosskranz. Although the minimum age for these cheeses is only three weeks, they are often aged out to five months.

ROUGE ET NOIR YELLOW BUCK CHEVRE

Marin French Cheese Company • Petaluma, CA

Chablis

Mixed herd

Bloomy rind
24 oz. disk
Pasteurized
Microbial coagulant
Affinage of 2 weeks
Available year-round
Creamery
Similar to Camembert

Marin French Cheese Company is a historical landmark in Marin County having produced French-style cheeses with milk from local dairies since 1865. The Rouge et Noir Yellow Buck Chevre is unique in that it uses a true Camembert culture unlike many Camembert-style goat cheeses that rely on other mold strains. The aroma is subtler than traditional Camembert and the paste has a light lactic flavor brightened by salty notes. The texture of the paste has a roux-like grit.

Marin French makes a blue version of this goat milk Camembert, Rouge et Noir Marin Chevre Blue, in which the subtle, cooked goat milk sweetness is offset by musty flavored blue veins. They also make a Camembert from a blend of cow and goat milk. This cheese, Mélange, is similar in texture to the Yellow Buck Chevre but with more rich, buttery flavors.

ROUSETTE

La Clarine Farm • Somerset, CA

IPA

Alpine

Washed rind
8–10 oz. wheel
Raw
Animal rennet
Affinage of 2 months
Available summer through mid-winter
Farmstead
Similar to chevrotin

The paste of this stout wheel carries robust flavors typical of washed rinds. This rich, beefiness is accented by salty and buttery notes. Rousette's texture is semi-soft and slightly tacky to the touch. Younger wheels may be chalky at the center.

SAINT HELENS

Port Madison Farm • Bainbridge Island, WA

Sancerre

Nubian

Surface-ripened
3–8 oz. pyramid
Pasteurized
Microbial coagulant
Affinage of 2 weeks
Available late spring through early winter
Farmstead
Similar to Valençay

Named for one of Washington's famous volcanoes, Saint Helens is greeted with a dusting of ash after it comes out of its pyramid form. Over a period of two weeks, a combination of molds covers the ash by developing a thin white coat on the surface. The fluffy, moist interior is slightly less tangy than fresh chèvre. Subtle notes of hay linger on the rind.

SAINT OLGA

Rivers Edge Chèvre • Logsden, OR

Stout

Alpine

Semi-firm
3.5–4 lb. wheel
Raw
Animal rennet
Affinage of 3 months
Available year-round
Farmstead
Similar to Capra Valtellina

Saint Olga has a supple, peachy-colored rind when it is young because it is washed throughout its development with Oatmeal Cream Stout from local Siletz Brewery. Once the wheels are washed less frequently, the rind takes on a mottled gray-brown hue. The paste is firm but remains pliable and is marked by small pinholes throughout. Initial flavors are herbal and woodsy followed by a lingering note of dulce de leche on the finish.

SALLY JACKSON GOAT CHEESE WRAPPED IN GRAPE LEAVES

Sally Jackson Cheeses • Oroville, WA

Chinon

Nubian and Alpine

Semi-soft
2 lb. wheel
Raw
Animal rennet
Affinage of 2 months
Available late spring through fall
Farmstead
Similar to Banon

This cheese is made with milk from Sally Jackson's farmstead herd of fewer than twenty Nubians and Alpines. The cheeses are semi-soft, left in forms to drain through gravity only, and develop a pudgy texture when fully ripe. The wheels, which ripen from the outside inward, grow a mottled, sometimes grizzly-looking skin beneath the grape-leaf wrapping. Flavors are dominated by vibrant acidity and herbaceous goat milk with a nuttiness in the background.

SALLY JACKSON SHEEP CHEESE WRAPPED IN CHESTNUT LEAVES

Sally Jackson Cheeses • Oroville, WA

Scotch

East Friesian, Suffolk, and Romanov

Semi-soft
2 lb. wheel
Raw
Animal rennet
Affinage of 2 months
Available summer through fall
Farmstead
Similar to Reblochon

Sally Jackson turns her flock of nearly thirty sheep out onto pasture daily, milks them, and transforms all that milk into this cheese. The aptly-named, unpressed wheels are wrapped in chestnut leaves. The paste is semi-soft and springy in texture, somehow moist without being creamy on the palate. This cheese displays a lovely, sweet sheep milk flavor, alongside muted sour cream notes.

SAN ANDREAS

Bellwether Farms • Petaluma, CA

Montepulciano

East Friesian and Lacaune

Semi-firm
3.5 lb. wheel
Raw
Animal rennet
Affinage of 3 months
Available year-round
Farmstead and Creamery
Similar to young pecorino

This cheese was developed after the producer's bout of travel and research in Italy, home to many outstanding pecorinos. An important step in making this cheese is cutting the curds down to the size of peas. After the curds are scooped into forms they are not pressed (beyond the force of gravity), instead the cutting and stirring of these small curds encourages them to release as much whey as possible before they are hooped. Once in their forms, the wheels are turned every fifteen minutes for the first two hours to foster even draining and a uniform shape. These newly formed wheels spend their initial evening in the aging room and are hand-salted the following morning. Although San Andreas is aged for just three months it develops small crunchy bits throughout the paste, a characteristic more common in older cheeses. It has a balanced combination of fresh milk and toasted nut flavors.

SAN JOAQUIN GOLD

Fiscalini Farmstead Cheese Company • Modesto, CA

Côtes du Rhône

Holstein

Semi-firm
32 lb. wheel
Raw
Microbial coagulant
Affinage of 16 months
Available year-round
Farmstead
Validus Certified Responsible Producer
Similar to Montasio

San Joaquin Gold is an American original with a great story. John Fiscalini's first cheesemaker worked with him to develop a cheese in the likeness of the Italian classic, fontina. Upon arriving on the farm, cheesemaker Mariano Gonzalez tried the cheese and said, though wonderful, it was nothing like fontina. Fiscalini followed his suggestion to change the name of this unique cheese to reflect the region in which it is made. The same basic recipe is still followed but at the end of the process the wheels are pressed more, yielding a semi-firm paste with clean brown butter flavors.

SAUVETERRE

Monteillet Fromagerie • Dayton, WA

Viognier

East Friesian and Lacaune

Semi-firm
6 lb. wheel
Raw
Microbial coagulant
Affinage of 2 months
Available late fall through winter
Farmstead
Similar to Corsican sheep tomme

The producer generally makes these wheels toward the end of the sheep milking season. With that timing, and a little aging in the cellar, they are ready to sell during the months when there isn't any fresh sheep milk, and eventually goat milk, for cheesemaking. Sauveterre is made entirely from sheep milk so classic fatty, nutty, and earthy flavors shine through in the paste. On the rare occasions that wheels are allowed to age beyond four to five months, they develop small, crunchy tyrosine crystals in the paste.

10 SCIO HERITAGE

Ancient Heritage Dairy • Scio, OR

Irouléguy

Lacaune–East Friesian cross

Semi-firm
5 lb. wheel
Raw
Animal rennet
Affinage of 3 months
Available summer through mid-fall
Farmstead
Similar to Ros Ombra

The inspiration for this 100 percent sheep milk tomme comes from Spain, home of legendary cheeses like Manchego. Named for the Oregon town in which it is made, this semi-firm cheese has hearty and rustic flavors like roasted chestnuts and hazelnuts. Because it is aged only three months, it retains more moisture, a refreshing lactic acidity, and a somewhat bendy texture contrary to some Manchegos and pecorinos that become dry and crumbly.

SEASCAPE

Central Coast Creamery • Oakdale, CA

 *Amber*

 *Holstein*

 *Mixed herd*

Semi-soft
9 lb. wheel
Pasteurized
Microbial coagulant
Affinage of 6 months
Available year-round
Creamery
Similar to goat Gouda

Seascape's wonderful balance of savory and sweet flavors contributes to its popular appeal. The combination of goat and cow milk gives it a light caramel flavor that is ballasted by a refreshing tang. A lovely way to enjoy Seascape is atop toasted slices of hearty bread or crisp crackers studded with fruits and nuts.

SEASTACK

Mount Townsend Creamery • Port Townsend, WA

 *Old world pinot noir*

 *Holstein*

Bloomy rind
7 oz. drum
Pasteurized
Animal rennet
Affinage of 15–18 days
Available year-round
Creamery
Similar to Neufchâtel

Double stacked rounds of cow milk curd are separated with a layer of ash, coated with ash, and then encouraged to develop a thin, soft bloomy rind. The interior remains velvety and displays a fresh, milky flavor up front. Directly beneath the rind, the paste is a bit thicker and tastes of mushrooms and salt. As the cheese ages, the rind can develop a peppery bite.

SERENA

Three Sisters Farmstead Cheese • Lindsay, CA

Ale

Jersey

Hard
20 lb. wheel
Raw
Microbial coagulant
Affinage of 1 year
Available year-round
Farmstead
Similar to aged provolone

Bandaged in cheesecloth and designed to be aged for a minimum of one year, the paste of this cheese has a surprisingly smooth texture and intense, sharp flavor. The owners of this farmstead operation are third-generation dairy farmers working with a herd of Jerseys in the San Joaquin Valley, California's most productive agricultural area. Rotating animals on pasture is challenging in this region because of steep land prices and weather conditions, so the animals are mainly housed in ventilated free stalls with access to a large exercise pen.

SERENITA

Three Sisters Farmstead Cheese • Lindsay, CA

Arneis

Jersey

Semi-firm
20 lb. wheel
Raw
Microbial coagulant
Affinage of 2 months
Available year-round
Farmstead
Similar to Beaufort crossed with Parmesan

A smooth, natural rind develops over these large wheels during the minimum two-month aging period. The flavors resemble the slightly fermented, white wine sweetness of Swiss mountain-style cheeses and the texture is creamy on the palate. The curds are not cooked so Serenita keeps a bit more moisture than many mountain-style cheeses.

SHEPHERD

Yerba Santa Goat Dairy • Lakeport, CA

Belgian white

French Alpine, Saanen, and LaMancha

Semi-firm
5 lb. wheel
Raw
Microbial coagulant
Affinage of 5 months
Available fall through winter
Farmstead
Similar to Gouda crossed with Parmesan

Cheesemaker Javier Salmon grew up working in his family's cheese plant in Peru and is carrying on the tradition of South American dairying practices and cheese recipes. Shepherd is an example of a European-style cheese made at the dairy, with milk from their herd of seventy-five goats. Wheels are allowed to develop a natural rind during their five months of aging. The texture is firm and the paste has flavors of mild, milky caramel and finishes with a small bite.

SHEPHERD'S GEM

Larkhaven Farmstead Cheese • Tonasket, WA

Marsanne

East Friesian crossed with several breeds

Semi-firm
3–4 lb. wheel
Raw
Animal rennet
Affinage of 5 months
Available late fall through winter
Creamery
Similar to Ossau-Vieille

A favorite saying of the cheesemaker at Larkhaven is: "We will sell no cheese before its time." This credo is perfectly exemplified by this tomme as it is aged anywhere from five to seven months, depending on how the wheels develop. The paste is firm but has enough moisture to maintain a pliable texture. Shepherd's Gem is dominated by the sweeter, nutty flavors (think Oloroso sherry) common in Pyrenees-style sheep tommes, and accented by tangy, lactic notes.

SIERRA MOUNTAIN TOMME

La Clarine Farm • Somerset, CA

Vin de Savoie

Alpine

Semi-firm
3.5 lb. wheel
Raw
Animal rennet
Affinage of 2 months
Available summer through mid-winter
Farmstead
Similar to Tomme de Savoie

Located approximately seventy-five miles due east of Sacramento, La Clarine Farm is squarely in the foothills of California's Sierra Nevada. This semi-firm tomme showcases woodsy, forest floor flavors that are evocative of the rugged outdoors or a damp cellar. A noticeable dose of salt and hints of butter round out the savory bouquet. As the wheels age, the paste beneath the rind shifts from bone-white to pale brown, like the color of dried hay.

SILETZ RIVER DRUM

Rivers Edge Chèvre • Logsden, OR

Pouilly Fumé

Alpine

Bloomy rind
3.5–4.5 oz. drum
Pasteurized
Animal rennet
Affinage of 15 days
Available year-round
Farmstead
Similar to chevrot and crottin

Siletz River Drums, and the smaller Siletz River Stones, are riffs on the traditional crottin. Both sizes are made from pre-drained curds; before curds are packed into the appropriate-sized forms they are left in cloth bags to drain overnight. Once the cheeses are shaped, they begin the two-week aging cycle during which their exteriors form a wrinkly skin. This skin is primarily developed by the yeast *Geotrichum*, which is combined with other molds to achieve the desired flavor and properly break down the paste beneath. Both the Drums and the Stones remain somewhat dense and firm—their pastes dry out and tighten over time as opposed to breaking down into a more liquidy or creamy texture.

SILLY BILLY

River Valley Cheese • Fall City, WA

Beaujolais

Mixed herd

Washed rind
2 lb., 4 lb., 8 lb., or 10 lb. wheel
Raw
Microbial coagulant
Affinage of 3 months
Available year-round
Farmstead
Similar to Murcia al Vino (Drunken Goat)

River Valley Cheese's mixed herd of ninety-six goats are on pasture for approximately seven months of the year. The herd is kept in confinement during the remaining months because of the wet weather and lack of pasture. This goat tomme comes in a variety of wheel sizes, all of which are washed in Rockridge Orchard's Raspberry Port and aged for a minimum of three months. Though the wheels age slightly differently depending on size, they all boast an assertive fruity flavor and supple texture.

SILVER MOUNTAIN AGED CLOTHBOUND CHEDDAR

Bravo Farms • Traver, CA

Brown or red ale

Holstein

Semi-firm
13 lb. or 20 lb. wheels
Raw
Microbial coagulant
Affinage of 1 year
Available year-round
Creamery
Similar to New England Clothbound Cheddar

This Cheddar has a dense and clay-like texture, a result of being made in the traditional English clothbound-style. Though the cheese can crumble a bit when cut, the paste still feels moist on the palate. The producers initially milked their own cows but have since opted to sell their herd and focus on cheesemaking; they now purchase Holstein milk from a dairy farm a couple miles down the road. Classic flavors of sharp Cheddar are complimented by aromas of damp cellar. Silver Mountain is delicious with a dollop of mango or banana chutney.

SKAGIT PARMESAN

Golden Glen Creamery • Bow, WA

Cremant de Bourgogne

Guernsey and Holstein

Semi-firm
2 lb. or 13 lb. wheel
Pasteurized
Microbial coagulant
Affinage of 6 months
Available year-round
Farmstead
Similar to Sbrinz

Named after one of Washington's prime agricultural valleys, Skagit Parmesan is a semi-firm, natural-rind wheel that has been rubbed down to prevent mold growth. The recipe is similar to that used for the famed Parmigiano-Reggiano but the cheesemaker at Golden Glen uses whole milk rather than the traditional skim milk. The resulting cheese is milder than the Italian version and filled with flavors of melted butter.

SMOKEY BLUE

Rogue Creamery • Central Point, OR

American whiskey

Brown Swiss, Holstein,
and Brown Swiss–Holstein cross

Blue
5 lb. wheel
Raw
Microbial coagulant
Affinage of 4 months
Available year-round
Creamery
Food Alliance Sustainable Producer

Smokey Blue is a riff on Rogue's flagship Oregon Blue. The creamery experimented with a variety of woods and finally settled on hazelnut shells, an abundant resource in their local area, over which the wheels are cold-smoked for more than twelve hours. The smokey flavor is subtle and melds well with the mild blue notes. The texture is slightly cakey though still quite dense.

SPRING CHEESE

Port Madison Farm • Bainbridge Island, WA

Pinot grigio

Nubian

Semi-soft
6 lb. wheel
Pasteurized
Microbial coagulant
Affinage of 2 months
Available in summer
Farmstead
Similar to Havarti

Though this cheese *is* the first one produced in the spring, it was named for its springy texture rather than the season. Spring Cheese is a semi-soft wheel in the style of Havarti that has mild flavors and no mold growth on the rind. The use of goat milk, instead of the more traditional cow milk, adds an earthy depth to the paste.

ST. GEORGE

Matos Cheese Factory • Santa Rosa, CA

Chardonnay

Mixed herd

Semi-firm
10–20 lb. wheel
Pasteurized
Microbial coagulant
Affinage of 7 months
Available year-round
Creamery
Similar to Sao Jorge

Joe Matos and his wife, Mary, moved to the United States from Sao Jorge, a small island in the Azores. Many families on that island had dairy cows and made a cheese called Sao Jorge. The Matos family brought the recipe for this cheese with them when they settled in Sonoma and they named it St. George in honor of its place of origin.

After the curds are cut, they are stirred by hand for a period of time before being scooped into their large forms. The wheels are pressed and then popped out onto shelves in the aging room. The golden yellow paste, pocked with small openings, has hints of onion and a slight fermented flavor that recalls Emmentaler.

ST. PAT

Cowgirl Creamery • Petaluma, CA

White Burgundy

Holstein, Jersey,
and Holstein-Jersey cross

Bloomy rind
10 oz. drum
Pasteurized
Microbial coagulant
Affinage of 4 weeks
Available spring through summer
Creamery
Certified Organic
Similar to Caerphilly crossed with Camembert

Due to weather conditions along the northern California coastline, the herd that supplies the milk for this cheese cannot be on pasture beyond mid-autumn. St. Pat is made in celebration of the cows returning to pasture in early spring. Each small wheel is wrapped in the leaves of stinging nettles which have been blanched to deactivate their sting. This wrapping imparts a subtle vegetal flavor to a paste dominated by sour cream notes. As the cheese ripens, the crumbly interior is transformed into a silken paste.

SUBBLIME

Estrella Family Creamery • Montesano, WA

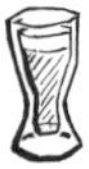

IPA

Primarily LaMancha

Primarily Normandy

Bloomy rind
8 oz. disk
Raw
Animal rennet
Affinage of 2 months
Available spring through fall
Farmstead
Similar to Constant Bliss

The curds are formed into low, wide disks with a finished height of approximately one inch. This shape creates a lot of surface area so the bacteria developing on the rind have a faster impact on the paste. The rind is riddled with irregular indentations and has a touch of bloomy growth. The wheels, made entirely from goat milk or with a blend of goat and cow milk, are generally semi-soft and have a clay-like paste, though the texture can vary to semi-firm. Unlike many bloomy rind cheeses, Subblime doesn't become overly peppery or sharp when it ages beyond the semi-soft texture.

SUMI

Goat's Leap • Saint Helena, CA

Sancerre

LaMancha

Surface-ripened
8–10 oz. truncated pyramid
Pasteurized
Animal rennet
Affinage of 10 days
Available year-round
Farmstead
Similar to Valençay

Resembling a classic French goat milk cheese called Valençay, Sumi is a sturdy, truncated pyramid coated with vegetable ash. A thin, wrinkly white skin develops over the course of its affinage. The paste is tangy and lactic. Near the rind, the cakey texture verges on liquidy.

SUNSET BAY

Rivers Edge Chèvre • Logsden, OR

Sauvignon blanc

Alpine

Bloomy rind
2 lb. wheel
Pasteurized
Animal rennet
Affinage of 15 days
Available year-round
Farmstead
Similar to aged Valençay

The bright orange-red line of Spanish pimentón in the middle of these wheels is intended to capture the appearance of the sky at Sunset Bay, a spot on the Oregon coast near Rivers Edge Chèvre. The outside of each wheel is covered with vegetable ash, gradually developing from a delicate bloom into a rind. Over time, the paste becomes runny directly beneath the rind but the innermost part remains velvety and light.

SWEET DREAMS

Fairview Farm • Dallas, OR

Pale ale

Alpine, Nubian, and Alpine-Nubian cross

Semi-soft
2–4 lb. wheel
Raw
Microbial coagulant
Affinage of 2 months
Available summer through winter
Farmstead
Animal Welfare Approved
Similar to Twig Farm Goat Tomme

The small goat herd at Fairview Farm is sent out to browse shrubs and brush from the Applegate Trail, which is used by ranchers running livestock as a detour around challenging parts of the Columbia River. This foraged feed, supplementary to the goats' steady diet of organic hay and locally milled grain, definitely has an impact on the milk. The tall, basket-molded Sweet Dreams have herbaceous flavors mixed with hints of pomace. The paste is riddled with small openings but the texture comes together on the tongue.

Fairview also makes a small, one- and a half-pound tommette called Cynthian. The addition of a bouquet of rosemary, sage, chives, and oregano to these compact, natural-rinded wheels accents the existing earthy notes in the paste

SWISS

Rosecrest Farm • Chehalis, WA

IPA

Milking Shorthorn

Semi-firm
8–11 lb. wheel
Raw
Animal rennet
Affinage of 3 months
Available year-round
Farmstead
Certified Organic
Similar to Emmentaler

The rinds of these wheels are rubbed down continuously throughout the three-month affinage to prevent any mold growth. The outcome is a smooth, blond wheel of Swiss cheese made with milk from Milking Shorthorns. The slightly sweeter flavor in this breed's milk is perceptible in the cheese, balancing out the tongue-stinging bite characteristic of Emmentaler-style cheeses.

TAUPINIÈRE

Laura Chenel's Chevre • Sonoma, CA

Seyssel

Mixed herd

Surface-ripened
9 oz. drum
Pasteurized
Microbial coagulant
Affinage of 12–14 days
Available year-round
Creamery
Similar to Neufchâtel

These small, dome-topped drums are sprinkled with vegetable ash and sprayed with a special combination of molds so that they will develop soft white rinds. The paste has the lightly acidic quality of young goat cheese and a mellow milky flavor in the background. The texture is light and airy and the rind is a bit toothsome.

TOMA

Vella Cheese Company • Sonoma, CA

Nebbiolo

Holstein and Guernsey

Semi-soft
10 lb. wheel
Pasteurized
Microbial coagulant
Affinage of 1 month
Available year-round
Creamery
Similar to Italian Toma

The name Toma is used somewhat broadly by Italians to describe cow milk cheeses that range from soft to semi-firm. The Toma produced by Vella Cheese Company is a large, soft, pudgy wheel that is slightly ripened. The exterior is just a bit tougher than the paste rather than developing a natural rind of various molds. Sweet aromas of fermentation are present in the paste; when wheels are aged to three months, the dominant yeasty flavor finishes with a touch of sharpness.

TOME DU CORBIER

Shamrock Artisan Goat Cheese • Willits, CA

Old world syrah

Purebred Alpine, Nubian, and LaMancha

Semi-firm
3–5 lb. wheel
Pasteurized
Microbial coagulant
Affinage of 10 weeks
Available year-round
Farmstead
Similar to Picodon

Slightly inland, about halfway between the old growth Redwoods and the Bay Area, this farmstead producer makes a pure goat milk wheel that has a dense texture. Once the wheels come out of their forms and have a chance to dry a bit on the outside, they are sealed in plastic before moving into the aging room. The seal prevents the growth of molds on the rind and also preserves more moisture than if the wheels were fully exposed to air. The cheese develops intense herbal and red currant flavors at the center and becomes piquant at the rind.

TOMME DE CUIVREE

Goldin Artisan Goat Cheese • Molalla, OR

Vin de Savoie

Primarily Alpine

Washed rind
3.25–3.75 lb. wheel
Raw
Animal rennet
Affinage of 2 months
Available late spring through early winter
Farmstead
Similar to Twig Farm Soft Wheel

These wheels have a rust-colored rind as a result of repeated washings with *Brevibacterium linens*. The bacteria on the rind transform the interior from stiff and cakey into a smooth paste and release pungent and savory cream flavors. The goats at this farmstead creamery are dried off for a couple months in the winter which leads to a small lapse in the availability of this cheese.

TOMME DE SAWTELL

Goldin Artisan Goat Cheese • Molalla, OR

Oregon pinot noir

Primarily Alpine

Semi-firm
3.25–3.75 lb. wheel
Raw
Animal rennet
Affinage of 2 months
Available late spring through early winter
Farmstead
Similar to Ticklemore

This handsome, dark brown and gray matte-rinded tomme is made entirely of raw goat milk from Carine Goldin's small herd. The paste is a dull white color and pocked throughout with small holes. Flavors of fresh sweet goat milk and delicate forest floor notes are enhanced by a small bite on the finish.

TRAILHEAD

Mount Townsend Creamery • Port Townsend, WA

Amber

Jersey

Semi-firm
6 lb. wheel
Pasteurized
Animal rennet
Affinage of 4 months
Available year-round
Creamery
Similar to Montasio crossed with Tomme de Savoie

Trailhead encapsulates an incredibly fresh, pure cheese flavor. Also detected are notes of milk, hints of sour cream, and a measured dose of salt. The curds are scooped into forms and pressed for a number of hours before soaking in a brine solution. Once they enter the aging rooms, the wheels are washed with a mixture of brine and yeast for the first two months. This washing aids in the development of a natural rind and also helps to maintain some moisture. Wheels are often released at four months; those carried out to six months begin to develop nutty flavors.

TRUFFLE TREMOR

Cypress Grove Chevre • Arcata, CA

Asti Spumante

Mixed herd

Surface-ripened
3 lb. wheel
Pasteurized
Microbial coagulant
Affinage of 3 weeks
Available year-round
Creamery
Similar to Robiola with truffles

These fuzzy wheels are entirely bone-white save for the dusty black bits of truffle scattered throughout the paste. Familiar, tangy, and fresh flavors of goat cheese balance the rustic, earthy, freshly dug potato notes of truffles. The texture is dense and clay-like on the palate and the thin, white rind has a slight snap.

TULARE CANNONBALL

Bravo Farms • Traver, CA

Pale ale

Jersey

Semi-firm
4 lb. ball
Raw
Microbial coagulant
Affinage of 6 months
Available year-round
Creamery
Similar to Edam

Made from a recipe for Edam, the flavor of this cheese is a cross between the fermented sweetness of Emmentaler and the fudgy texture of young Gouda. Tulare Cannonball is formed into Edam's characteristic ball shape and dipped in yellow-colored wax coating. The waxed rind helps the paste retain moisture during the six-month aging period.

TUMALO TOMME

Juniper Grove Farm • Redmond, OR

Valpolicella

Mixed herd

Semi-firm
3.5 lb. wheel
Raw
Microbial coagulant
Affinage of 2 months
Available year-round
Farmstead
Similar to Capra Valtellina

Tumalo Tomme (pronounced two-muh-low) is a mountain-style cheese which has a fruity, yeasty aroma. The curds are cut quite small and then stirred to release even more moisture. The paste has small openings throughout and finishes with a sharp bite. During their two-month affinage, the wheels are rubbed with brine and stacked on planks of pine; this wood is ideal because it doesn't transfer any flavors to the cheese.

TWO-FACED BLUE

Willapa Hills Farmstead Cheese • Doty, WA

Sauternes

Jersey and Holstein

East Friesian and Lacaune

Blue
10 lb. wheel
Raw
Animal rennet
Affinage of 3 months
Available late summer through fall
Creamery
Similar to Bleu de Basque

The sheep milk in these wheels comes from Willapa's own flock and the cow milk is produced by their neighbor's herd of Jerseys and Holsteins. Mixing sheep and cow milk for blue cheese production yields a combination of the thick and rich texture of Roquefort, a sheep milk classic, and the fudgy quality of cow milk blue king Stilton. The blue veins of Two-Faced Blue have a prevailing earthy flavor that blends well with the full-bodied cream notes in the paste. Willapa Hills also produces a longer aged version called Saggio which is available in mid-fall through winter. The six-month old wheels can develop more intense flavors and the blue molds can become peppery.

TWO ROCK VALLEY CHEESE

Two Rock Valley • Petaluma, CA

Merlot

Nubian

Semi-firm
13 lb. wheel
Raw
Microbial coagulant
Affinage of 2 months
Available year-round
Farmstead
Similar to Ubriaco

These sturdy goat milk tommes have a semi-firm texture and a paste that can verge on crumbly when cut. Earthy, cellar aromas are released when the wheels are cracked open. The paste tastes bright and fruity (think Beaujolais nouveau) and has a lovely goaty finish. Wheels can be released as early as two months but the cheesemaker also sells wheels that have been aged for one year.

UFO

Quillisascut Cheese Company • Rice, WA

Muscat

Primarily Alpine

Semi-soft
4–6 lb. wheel
Raw
Animal rennet
Affinage of 3 months
Available summer through winter
Farmstead
Similar to Monte Enebro

The producers use a rapid coagulation and then do not add any heat throughout the rest of the cheesemaking process. This technique gives UFO its unusual dry and firm texture that becomes very moist once it reaches the tongue. The name stands for unidentified fermented object which gives some indication of the wildness happening on the rind (what looks like the growth of blue mold is actually a variety of molds). The cheese has a big bouquet of flavors ranging from blue mold and yeast to sour cream.

UP IN SMOKE

Rivers Edge Chèvre • Logsden, OR

IPA

Alpine

Fresh
4 oz. ball
Pasteurized
Animal rennet
Affinage of 1 week
Available year-round
Farmstead
Similar to Cabécou Feuille

The technique of wrapping small rounds and disks of goat cheese in all sorts of leaves is common in most areas where goat cheese is produced. The leaves used for Up in Smoke are directly harvested from the Rivers Edge Chèvre farm. Big leaf and vine maple leaves are the primary type; when those run thin they switch to Salal, an evergreen shrub indigenous to the Pacific Northwest. Leaves are gathered and smoked over hickory and alder chips before being softened in bourbon. This modest soaking makes the leaves pliable enough to wrap around the small balls of fresh chèvre, which are then gently smoked over the same chips. The affinage is a scant week though the cheeses can be consumed for up to six weeks as the smoking acts as a mild preservative.

VACHE DE VASHON

Sea Breeze Farm • Vashon Island, WA

Pinot noir

Mixed herd

Semi-firm
2 lb. wheel
Raw
Animal rennet
Affinage of 2 months
Available year-round
Farmstead
Similar to Tomme de Savoie

Vache de Vashon (cow of Vashon) is a rugged, full-flavored tomme made from unpasteurized cow milk. The producer does not add any secondary cultures during the cheesemaking process, relying instead on the naturally occurring bacteria within the milk to develop texture and flavors in the cheese. Though this process allows for the development of unique cheeses, it also yields slightly less predictable outcomes than cheeses that use pasteurized milk and cheese-specific cultures. Vache de Vashon generally has a dense, semi-firm texture, and dominant vegetal and lactic flavors with a hint of barnyard.

VALENTINA

Estrella Family Creamery • Montesano, WA

Brown ale

Primarily Normandy

Semi-firm
10 lb. wheel
Raw
Animal rennet
Affinage of 6 months
Available year-round
Farmstead
Similar to Gruyère crossed with young Cheddar

These wheels are made to resemble the great Swiss mountain-style cheese Gruyère. The curds are cut, cooked, poured into forms, and then pressed to create a smooth and bendable paste. Each wheel is washed throughout its development with a combination of brine and select bacteria. The paste has some of the fermented fruity flavors associated with Swiss-style cheeses, but the acidity harkens to flavors found in traditional Cheddar wheels and makes Valentina unique.

During the Pacific Northwest's truffle season, Kelli Estrella makes a truffle-studded version of Valentina called Bea Truffled. The truffled wheels must age for months and are usually released in May.

VALENTINE

Ancient Heritage Dairy • Scio, OR

Champagne

Lacaune-East Friesian cross

Bloomy rind
3–5 oz. drum
Pasteurized
Animal rennet
Affinage of 3 weeks
Available late spring through mid-fall
Farmstead
Similar to La Tur crossed with Explorateur

This cheese is made seasonally, seven to eight months of the year, by a small farmstead producer. Their flock of sheep feed primarily on pasture, weather permitting, during their lactation which runs from April through November. Using sheep milk to make this bloomy rind cheese gives the paste a fatty and velvety texture. Without ever getting too funky, the flavors of damp hay and barnyard provide a great depth to Valentine.

VALLEY DOE

River Valley Cheese • Fall City, WA

Red ale

Mixed herd

Semi-soft
2 lb., 4 lb., 8 lb., or 10 lb. wheel
Raw
Microbial coagulant
Affinage of 70 days
Available year-round
Farmstead
Similar to Chevrotin des Bauges

These goat milk tommes are allowed to develop a natural rind but most molds are discouraged so it maintains a tough, straw-colored exterior. The bone-white paste beneath the rind has a pliable texture and a subtle grainy quality on the tongue. The bright and slightly acidic notes associated with fresh goat cheese are balanced by musty aromas and flavors of earth and light caramel.

VALLEY GIRL

River Valley Cheese • Fall City, WA

Pale ale

Brown Swiss

Semi-soft
2 lb., 4 lb., 8 lb. or 10 lb. wheel
Raw
Microbial coagulant
Affinage of 70 days
Available year-round
Farmstead
Similar to Toma

This tomme is modeled after the rustic, alpine cheeses of Europe. The paste is semi-soft and dominated by a pure butter flavor. A hint of dry hay is present in the thick, fudgy paste that melts on the tongue.

VALSETZ

Rivers Edge Chèvre • Logsden, OR

Sancerre

Alpine

Bloomy rind
9–10 oz. log
Pasteurized
Animal rennet
Affinage of 15 days
Available year-round
Farmstead
Similar to Saint Maure

Reminiscent of Saint Maure, a Loire Valley goat milk specialty, Valsetz is made in a log-shaped form. The curds are ladled directly into these forms and left to drain. Once they go into the aging room they begin to develop a fluffy bloom that covers them entirely. A cross-section of this log, or buche, as they call it in France, would show a velvety textured center and a ring of dense, smooth paste encapsulated by a soft, white rind. The purity of flavor in this young goat milk cheese is a tribute to the health of the farm's herd and the quality of their feed, a combination of foraged coastal browse and carefully selected, dried alfalfa.

VIKING

Washington State University Creamery • Pullman, WA

Red ale

Holstein

Semi-firm
30 oz. wheel
Pasteurized
Microbial coagulant
Affinage of 4 months
Available year-round
Creamery
Similar to Monterey Jack

Modeled on the recipe for jack cheese, Viking is high-moisture, pliable, and mild. Viking makes up only a small part of the overall cheese production at the WSU Creamery. This cheese is also made in a variety of flavors; all are packaged in the traditional tin cans that have become the signature of the creamery since they were invented there in the 1930s.

WEEBLES

Estrella Family Creamery • Montesano, WA

Barbera

Primarily Normandy

Semi-firm
2 lb. pear shape
Raw
Animal rennet
Affinage of 5 months
Available year-round
Farmstead
Similar to smoked caciocavallo

The paste of Weebles is quite smooth unlike many fibrous-feeling pasta filata-style cheeses, containing only hints of those sinewy strands of curd. The pear-shaped cheeses are smoked with alder wood and a delicate smokiness comes through on the paste. These cheese teardrops are tied together in twos and hung to age in the cellar like pairs of cheese mittens.

WHITE ROSE

Port Madison Farm • Bainbridge Island, WA

Old world pinot noir

Nubian

Bloomy rind
5–6 oz. disk
Pasteurized
Microbial coagulant
Affinage of 2 weeks
Available spring through fall
Farmstead
Similar to Brie

Cheesemaker Steve Phillips set out to make a cheese with the flavor profile of Brie that was portable enough to be packed up and eaten during a hike or on a picnic. A Brie made from goat milk, and especially one that can be aged until it is firm, is quite unusual. White Rose can be enjoyed as early as two weeks but it can also be aged out considerably longer. When aged, the texture is firm, though fudgy rather than dry and hard. The paste has intense mushroom and butter flavors like a Brie reduction.

WILLAPA WHITE

Willapa Hills Farmstead Cheese • Doty, WA

Cremant de Bourgogne

East Friesian and Lacaune

Fresh
5 oz. button
Pasteurized
Microbial coagulant
No affinage
Available spring through early winter
Farmstead
Similar to fromage frais

This button of fresh sheep milk cheese looks nearly identical to a fresh goat milk crottin, except that it's just a shade darker than the bright white of goat milk. Willapa White is truly a fresh cheese with no affinage beyond draining before being wrapped.

WIMER WINTER

Pholia Farm • Rogue River, OR

Savennières

Nigerian Dwarf

Washed rind
1.5 lb. wheel
Raw
Microbial coagulant
Affinage of 3 months
Available winter through early spring
Farmstead
Similar to Durrus

Gianaclis Caldwell, the cheesemaker at Pholia Farm, only makes this cheese in the fall and winter when humidity in their aging room is ideal for a washed rind cheese. The wheels of Wimer Winter are not as tall as some of Pholia's other tommes; this increases the surface area to paste ratio which allows the rind's bacteria to break down fats and proteins in as much of the paste as possible. The aroma of the paste is incredibly nutty, some of which comes through in the flavor. Also noticeable are understated woodsy notes, some natural goat's milk acidity, and a touch of pungency from the rind. The texture becomes semi-soft as the wheels reach maturity.

WYNOOCHEE RIVER BLUE

Estrella Family Creamery • Montesano, WA

Late harvest riesling

Primarily Normandy

Blue
5 lb. wheel
Raw
Animal rennet
Affinage of 2 months
Available year-round
Farmstead
Similar to Bayley Hazen Blue

Pronounced why-new-chee, these wheels are named for the river valley where the Estrella's farm is located. This blue tomme is hand-assembled with curds from two different milkings during the day. The wheels develop a natural rind but the outlines of the large curds are still visible. The texture is almost firm but quickly melts down on the tongue to become creamy. The blue mold has a dusty earthiness that mixes well with the sweet cream flavors in the milk.

YAQUINA BAY PAVÉ

Rivers Edge Chèvre • Logsden, OR

Cava

Alpine

Bloomy rind
19 oz. brick
Pasteurized
Animal rennet
Affinage of 15 days
Available year-round
Farmstead
Similar to Neufchâtel

This brick-shaped cheese is made from pre-drained curds which means that cheesemaking and cheese shaping happen at different times. Once the curds have drained in mesh bags they are pressed into a form and layered with green peppercorns. To ensure the shape will hold, the cheese is allowed to rest before being popped out of its form and placed in a cooler. A fuzzy, bloomy rind develops and the paste breaks down, from the outside in, into a smooth, creamy texture. Rivers Edge also makes an eight-ounce, square version called Euchre Mountain that is lined with black peppercorns through the middle and beneath its bloomy rind.

Cheesemakers

This section lists all of the West Coast cheesemakers that appear throughout the book, organized alphabetically within each state. Web sites, which are included whenever available, are generally the best source for up-to-date information about products, tours, and events.

CALIFORNIA

Achadinha Cheese Company
Petaluma, CA
www.achadinha.com
Mail order available

Andante Dairy
Petaluma, CA
www.andantedairy.com

Barinaga Ranch
Marshall, CA
www.barinagaranch.com

Belfiore Cheese Company
Berkeley, CA
www.belfiorecheese.com

Bellwether Farms
Petaluma, CA
www.bellwethercheese.com
Mail order available

Bodega Artisan Cheese
Bodega, CA
www.bodegaartisancheese.com
Mail order available
Tours by appointment only

Bohemian Creamery
Bodega, CA
www.bohemiancreamery.com

Bravo Farms
Traver, CA
www.bravofarms.com
Mail order available
Cheese shop open daily; cheese factory open Monday through Friday

Bubalus Bubalis
Gardena, CA
www.realmozzarella.com
Mail order available
Open to the public by appointment only

Central Coast Creamery
Oakdale, CA
www.centralcoastcreamery.com

Cowgirl Creamery
Petaluma, CA
www.cowgirlcreamery.com
Mail order available
Tours by appointment in Petaluma location; can view cheesemaking at the original facility in Point Reyes Station

Cypress Grove Chevre
Arcata, CA
www.cypressgrovechevre.com
Mail order available

Delice de la Vallee
Sonoma, CA
www.delicedelavalle.com

Fiscalini Farmstead Cheese Company
Modesto, CA
www.fiscalinicheese.com
Mail order available
Open to the public by appointment only

Gioia Cheese Company
South El Monte, CA
Retail outlet at production facility open Monday through Friday

Goat's Leap
Saint Helena, CA
www.goatsleap.com

Harley Farms
Pescadero, CA
www.harleyfarms.com
Mail order available
Farm tours and events scheduled regularly

Kendall Farms
Atascadero, CA
www.kendallfarmscremefraiche.com

La Clarine Farm
Somerset, CA
www.laclarinefarm.com

Laura Chenel's Chevre
Sonoma, CA
www.laurachenel.com

Loleta Cheese Factory
Loleta, CA
www.loletacheese.com
Mail order available
Retail store open daily

Marin French Cheese Company
Petaluma, CA
www.marinfrenchcheese.com
Mail order available
Retail store open and regularly scheduled tours daily

Matos Cheese Factory
Santa Rosa, CA
Retail store open daily.

Meyenberg Goat Milk Products
Turlock, CA
www.meyenberg.com
Mail order available

Midcoast Cheese Company
Los Banos, CA
www.franklinscheese.com

Nicolau Farms
Modesto, CA
www.nicolaufarms.com

North Valley Farms Chevre
Cottonwood, CA
www.northvalleyfarms.com
Mail order available

Oakdale Cheese
Oakdale, CA
www.oakdalecheese.com
Mail order available
Retail store open daily;
tours by appointment only

Pedrozo Dairy and Cheese Company
Orland, CA
www.realfarmsteadcheese.com

Point Reyes Farmstead Cheese Company
Point Reyes Station, CA
www.pointreyescheese.com
Mail order available
Tours by appointment only

Pug's Leap Farm
Healdsburg, CA
www.pugsleap.com

Redwood Hill Farm
Sebastopol, CA
www.redwoodhill.com
Mail order available
Annual open house and farm days

Rinconada Dairy
Santa Margarita, CA
www.rinconadadairy.com
Mail order available
Farm Stays and other scheduled events

Rumiano Cheese Company
Crescent City, CA
www.rumianocheese.com
Mail order available
Retail store open Monday through Saturday

Shamrock Artisan Goat Cheese
Willits, CA
www.shamrockartisan-goatcheese.com

Sierra Nevada Cheese Company
Willows, CA
www.sierranevadacheese.com

Spring Hill Cheese Company
Petaluma, CA
www.springhillcheese.com
Mail order available
Retail store open daily

Three Sisters Farmstead Cheese
Lindsay, CA
www.threesisterscheese.com
Tours by appointment only

Two Rock Valley
Petaluma, CA

Valley Ford Cheese
Valley Ford, CA
www.valleyfordcheeseco.com

Vella Cheese Company
Sonoma, CA
www.vellacheese.com
Mail order available
Retail store open Monday through Saturday; tours by appointment only

Winchester Cheese Company
Winchester, CA
www.winchestercheese.com
Mail order available

Yerba Santa Goat Dairy/ Bodega Goat Cheese
Lakeport, CA

OREGON

Alsea Acre Goat Cheese
Alsea, OR
www.home.earthlink.net/~luvsgoats/Alsea Acre/
Mail order available
Open to the public by appointment only

Ancient Heritage Dairy
Scio, OR
www.ancientheritagedairy.com

Fairview Farm
Dallas, OR
www.fairviewfarm.wordpress.com
Self-serve farm stand open daily

Ferns' Edge Goat Dairy
Lowell, OR
www.fernsedgedairy.com

Fraga Farm
Sweet Home, OR
www.fragafarm.com
Tours by appointment only

Goldin Artisan Goat Cheese
Molalla, OR
www.goldinartisangoatcheese.com
Mail order available

Jacobs Creamery
Canby, OR
www.jacobscreamery.com

Juniper Grove Farm
Redmond, OR
www.junipergrovefarm.com
Mail order available
Self-serve farm stand open Monday through Saturday; tours by appointment only

La Mariposa
Sweet Home, OR

New Moon Goat Dairy
Chiloquin, OR

Ochoa Cheese Factory
Eugene, OR

Pholia Farm
Rogue River, OR
www.pholiafarm.com
Mail order available
Open to the public the second Saturday of every month and every Monday; classes in animal husbandry and cheesemaking available by request

Rivers Edge Chèvre
Logsden, OR
www.threeringfarm.com
Mail order available
Open to the public by appointment only

Rogue Creamery
Central Point, OR
www.roguecreamery.com
Mail order available
Retail store open daily

Silver Falls Creamery
Salem, OR
www.silverfallscreamery.com
Mail order available

Siskiyou Crest Goat Dairy
Jacksonville, OR
Open to the public by appointment only

Tillamook County Creamery
Tillamook, OR
www.tillamookcheese.com
Mail order available
Visitor center open daily

Tumalo Farms
Bend, OR
www.tumalofarms.com
Mail order available
Open to the public by appointment only

Willamette Valley Cheese Company
Salem, OR
www.wvcheeseco.com
Open to the public by appointment only

WASHINGTON

Alpine Lakes Sheep Cheese
Leavenworth, WA
www.alpinelakescheese.com
Mail order available

Appel Farms
Ferndale, WA
www.appel-farms.com
Mail order available
Retail store open Monday through Saturday

Beecher's Handmade Cheese
Seattle, WA
www.beechershandmadecheese.com
Mail order available
Retail store open daily

Black Sheep Creamery
Adna, WA
www.blacksheepcreamery.com
Tours by appointment only

Blue Rose Dairy
Winlock, WA
www.bluerosedairy.com
Mail order available
Scheduled cheesemaking classes available; tours by appointment only

Dee Creek Farm
Woodland, WA
www.deecreekfarm.com

El Michoacano
Marysville, WA
Tours by appointment only

Estrella Family Creamery
Montesano, WA
www.estrellafamilycreamery.com
Farm store open Saturdays and by appointment

Golden Glen Creamery
Bow, WA
www.goldenglencreamery.com
Mail order available
Farm store open Monday through Saturday

Gothberg Farms
Bow, WA
www.gothbergfarms.com
Tours by appointment only

Grace Harbor Farms
Custer, WA
www.graceharborfarms.com
Farm store open Monday through Saturday

Larkhaven Farmstead Cheese
Tonasket, WA
www.larkhavenfarm.com
Tours by appointment only

Monteillet Fromagerie
Dayton, WA
www.monteilletcheese.com
Scheduled cheesemaking classes available; open weekends for tours and tastings

Mount Townsend Creamery
Port Townsend, WA
www.mttownsendcreamery.com
Mail order available
Creamery store open Wednesday through Sunday

Mystery Bay Farm
Nordland, WA
www.mysterybayfarm.com
Tours by appointment only

Pine Stump Farms
Omak, WA
www.pinestumpfarms.com
Country Weekends at the farm

Pleasant Valley Dairy
Ferndale, WA
Farm stand open Monday through Saturday (May to December); Saturday only (January to April)

Port Madison Farm
Bainbridge Island, WA

Quail Croft Farmstead Cheese
Friday Harbor, WA

Queseria Bendita
Yakima, WA
Retail shop open Monday through Friday

Quillisascut Cheese Company
Rice, WA
www.quillisascut.com
Classes and occasional tours available

River Valley Cheese
Fall City, WA
www.rivervalleycheese.com
Mail order available
Farm store open Saturdays; tours by appointment only

Rosecrest Farm
Chehalis, WA
www.rosecrestfarms.org
Mail order available
Open to the public

Sally Jackson Cheeses
Oroville, WA
www.sallyjacksoncheeses.com

Samish Bay Cheese Company
Bow, WA
www.samishbaycheese.com
Mail order available
Farm store open daily; tours by appointment only

Sea Breeze Farm
Vashon Island, WA
www.seabreezefarm.net

Silver Springs Creamery
Lynden, WA
www.silverspringscreamery.com
Mail order available
Farm store open daily

Steamboat Island Goat Farm
Olympia, WA
www.steamboatislandgoatfarm.com

Washington State University Creamery
Pullman, WA
www.wsu.edu/creamery/
Mail order available
Retail store open Monday through Friday

Willapa Hills Farmstead Cheese
Doty, WA
www.willapahills.com
Mail order available

Shops

Here is a list of some of the shops and markets around the country which offer a great selection of West Coast cheeses. As always, Web sites are the best source for current information.

Allyson's Kitchen
375 SW Powerhouse Drive
Bend, OR 97702
www.allysonskitchen.com

Artisanal Fromagerie and Bistro
2 Park Avenue
New York, NY 10016
www.artisanalbistro.com

Ashland Food CO-OP
237 North First Street
Ashland, OR 97520
www.ashlandfood.coop

Beecher's Handmade Cheese
1600 Pike Place
Seattle, WA 98101
www.beechershandmadecheese.com

Berkeley Bowl
2020 Oregon Street
Berkeley, CA 94703
www.berkeleybowl.com

Bi Rite
3639 18th Street
San Francisco, CA 94110
www.biritemarket.com

Big John's Market
1345 Healdsburg Avene
Healdsburg, CA 95448
www.bigjohnsmarket.com

California Wine and Cheese
115 West Foothill Boulevard
Monrovia, CA 91016
www.cawineandcheese.com

Central Market (Texas)
Multiple locations in Austin, TX and Dallas, TX
www.centralmarket.com

Central Market (Washington)
Multiple locations in Washington
www.central-market.com

C'est Cheese
825 Santa Barbara Street
Santa Barbara, CA 93101
www.cestcheese.com

Cheese and Crackers
238 Fourth Street
Yachats, OR 97498
www.cheeseandcrackersonline.com

Cheese Bar
6031 SE Belmont Street
Portland, OR 97215

Cheese Plus
2001 Polk Street
San Francisco, CA 94109
www.cheeseplus.com

Cowgirl Creamery (D.C.)
919 F Street NW
Washington, DC 20004
www.cowgirlcreamery.com

Cowgirl Creamery (Pt. Reyes Station)
80 Fourth Street
Point Reyes Station, CA 94956
www.cowgirlcreamery.com

Cowgirl Creamery (San Francisco)
1 Ferry Building #17
San Francisco, CA 94111
www.cowgirlcreamery.com

DeLaurenti Specialty Food and Wine
1435 First Avenue
Seattle, WA 98101
www.delaurenti.com

Di Bruno Brothers (Ninth Street)
930 South Ninth Street
Philadelphia, PA 19145
www.dibruno.com

Di Bruno Brothers (Chestnut)
1730 Chestnut Street
Philadelphia, PA 19103
www.dibruno.com

Di Raimondo's Italian Market Cheese Shop
822 13th Street
Paso Robles, CA 93446
www.pasocheese.com

Elephant's Delicatessen
Multiple locations in Portland, OR
www.elephantsdeli.com

Food Front (Hillsdale)
6344 SW Capitol Highway
Hillsdale Shopping Center
Portland, OR 97239
www.foodfront.coop

Food Front (Northwest)
2375 NW Thurman Street
Portland, Oregon 97210
www.foodfront.coop

Foster and Dobbs
2518 NE 15th Avenue
Portland, OR 97212
www.fosteranddobbs.com

King's Market
160 Spring Street
Friday Harbor, WA 98250
www.kings-market.com

Larry's Market
8737 North Deerwood Drive
Brown Deer, WI 53209
www.larrysmarket.com

Liberty Heights Fresh
1290 South 1100 East
Salt Lake City, UT 84152
www.libertyheightsfresh.com

Madison Market
1600 East Madison Street
Seattle, WA 98122
www.madisonmarket.com

Marche Provisions
296 East Fifth Avenue
Eugene, OR 97401
www.marcheprovisions.com

Marczyk Fine Foods
770 East 17th Avenue
Denver, CO 80203
www.marczykfinefoods.com

Market of Choice
Multiple locations in Ashland, Eugene, and Portland, OR
www.marketofchoice.com

Metropolitan Market
Multiple locations in Federal Way, Seattle, and Tacoma, WA
www.metropolitan-market.com

Mollie Stone's Market
Multiple locations in the California Bay Area
www.molliestones.com

Moscow Food CO-OP
121 East Fifth Street
Moscow, ID 83843
www.moscowfood.coop

Murray's Cheese Shop (Grand Central)
43rd Street and Lexington Avenue
New York, NY 10017
www.murrayscheese.com

Murray's Cheese Shop (Greenwich Village)
254 Bleeker Street
New York, NY 10014
www.murrayscheese.com

New Seasons Market
Multiple locations in Portland, Oregon
www.newseasonsmarket.com

Newport Avenue Market
1121 NW Newport Avenue
Bend, OR 97701
www.newportavemarket.com

Oakville Grocery Co. (Healdsburg)
124 Matheson Street
Healdsburg, CA 95448
www.oakvillegrocery.com

Oakville Grocery Co. (Napa Valley)
7856 St. Helena Highway
Oakville, CA 94562
www.oakvillegrocery.com

Olympia Food CO-OP
3111 Pacific Avenue SE
Olympia, WA 98501
www.olympiafood.coop/local

Oxbow Cheese Merchant
610 First Street
Napa, CA 94559
www.oxbowpublicmarket.com/tenants

Pastaworks
Multiple locations in
Portland, OR
www.pastaworks.com

Pastoral Artisan Cheese, Bread & Wine (East Lake)
53 East Lake Street
Chicago, IL 60601
www.pastoralartisan.com

Pastoral Artisan Cheese, Bread & Wine (North Broadway)
2945 North Broadway
Chicago, IL 60657
www.pastoralartisan.com

People's CO-OP
3029 SE 21st Avenue
Portland, OR 97202
www.peoples.coop

Quality Cheese
1508 Pike Place #B
Seattle, WA 98101

Quel Fromage
1200 Old Fairhaven Parkway, Ste. 101
Bellingham, WA 98225
www.quelfromage.com

Rainbow Grocery
1745 Folsom Street
San Francisco, CA 94103
www.rainbow.coop

Raymond & Co. Cheesemongers
Jack London Villlage
14301 Arnold Drive
Glen Ellen, CA 95442
www.raymondcheesemongers.com

Rogue Creamery Store
311 North Front Street
Central Point, OR 97502
www.roguecreamery.com

Saint James Cheese Company
5004 Prytania Street
New Orleans, LA 70118
www.stjamescheese.com

Salumiere Cesario
20 North 2nd Avenue
Walla Walla, WA 99362
www.salumierecesario.com

Saunders Cheese Market
210 South Washington Street
Spokane, WA 99201
www.saunderscheesemarket.com

Skagit Valley CO-OP
202 South First Street
Mount Vernon, WA 98273
www.skagitfoodcoop.com

Slough Food
5766 Cain's Court, Suite B
Edison, WA 98232
www.sloughfood.com

Square Deal Wine and Cheese
2321 NW Thurman Street
Portland, OR 97210
www.squaredealwine.com

The Cheese Cellar
100 Fourth Avenue North, Suite 150
Seattle, WA 98109
www.thecheesecellar.com

The Cheese Shop (Carmel)
Carmel Plaza,
Ocean and Junipero
Carmel, CA 93921
www.thecheeseshopinc.com

The Cheese Shop (Healdsburg)
423 Center Street
Healdsburg, CA 94119
www.sharpandnutty.com

The Cheeseboard Collective
1504 Shattuck Avenue
Berkeley, CA 94709
www.cheeseboardcollective.coop

The Horse Radish
211 West Main Street
Carlton, OR 97111
www.thehorseradish.com

The Pasta Shop (Berkeley)
1786 Fourth Street
Berkeley, CA 94710
www.pastashop.net

The Pasta Shop (Oakland)
5655 College Avenue
Oakland, CA 94618
www.rockridgemarkethall.com

The Resident Cheesemonger
405 Main Street
Edmonds, WA 98020
www.residentcheesemonger.com

Vella Cheese Company Store
315 Second Street East
Sonoma, CA 95476
www.vellacheese.com

Venissimo Cheese
Multiple locations in
Del Mar, Long Beach,
and San Diego, CA
www.venissimo.com

Vivant Fine Cheese
840 11th Street
Paso Robles, CA 93446
www.vivantfinecheese.com

Whole Foods
Locations nationwide
www.wholefoods.com

Woodlands Market
735 College Avenue
Kentfield, CA 94904
www.woodlandsmarket.com

Zingerman's
422 Detroit Street
Ann Arbor, MI 48104
www.zingermans.com

Zupan's
Multiple locations in
Portland, OR
www.zupans.com

Glossary

AFFINAGE. A French term that describes the aging or curing of cheese.

BREVIBACTERIUM LINENS. Bacteria that develop on the surface of specific cheeses and aid in breakdown of the paste and development of flavors. Known for imparting orange-brown hues and pungent aromas.

BRINING. Optional cheesemaking step in which the cheese is soaked in a saltwater solution.

CHÈVRE. The French word for goat and the name for fresh goat milk cheese.

COAGULANT. The substance used to accelerate the natural process of milk solids joining together to form curds.

COMPONENTS. The ratio in milk of solids (fats, proteins, and minerals) to water.

CONFINEMENT. A system in which animals are kept within the confines of a barn or penned-in area.

CREAMERY. Cheesemaking operation which uses milk purchased from a dairy farm rather than having a herd on site.

CURD. The solids within milk that clump together during cheesemaking.

FARMSTEAD. Cheesemaking operation in which cheesemakers use milk from their own herd on the same land where they make the cheese.

GEOTRICHUM. Mold or yeast used to develop the wrinkly skin-like rind usually found on smaller cheeses.

HALOIR. A slightly cool and low humidity room for drying cheese.

HOOPING. The process of scooping or pumping curds out of the vat into their molds or forms.

LACTATION. The period of time following the birth of young during which a mammal produces milk.

LACTIC COAGULATION. Relying on the activity of lactic bacteria that develop lactic acid to trigger coagulation.

LACTOSE. The naturally occurring sugar in milk.

PASTE. The interior of a cheese (everything except the rind).

PASTEURIZATION. The process of heating milk to a temperature hot enough to kill the bacteria.

PASTURE-BASED. A system in which animals feed on pasture whenever possible.

PENICILLIUM CANDIDUM. A species of mold used in the production of cheeses in which the development of a bloomy rind is desired, such as Brie and Camembert.

RAPID COAGULATION. Coagulation that is triggered or accelerated by the addition of animal rennet, or some form of microbial or plant coagulant.

RAW MILK CHEESE. Cheese made with milk that has not been heat-treated.

SEASONAL. Indicates that the cheesemaker only makes cheese during a specific part of the year; or that animals are only milked in a specific season, rather than year-round.

SECONDARY CULTURE. Often a combination of yeasts, molds, and bacteria, which perform specialized tasks throughout cheesemaking and affinage.

STARTER CULTURE. Bacteria added to the milk early in the cheesemaking process which work to convert lactose into lactic acid.

TRIPLE CREAM. A cheese that has more than 75 percent butterfat in its dry matter or approximately 40 percent overall butterfat.

TOMME. Cheeses that are most often shaped into wide, low wheels.

TYROSINE CRYSTALS. Clusters of the amino acid tyrosine scattered throughout the paste of some aged cheeses.

UNHOOPING. The process of removing drained and/or pressed cheeses from their forms.

WASHED CURD. An optional cheesemaking step in which a portion of the whey is drained away from the curds and replaced with water.

WHEY. Liquid portion of milk that separates from milk solids during cheesemaking.

WHEYING OFF. Draining the liquid portion (whey) from the solid curds.

Bibliography

Barthelemy, Roland, and Arnaud Sperat-Czar. 2003. *Guide du Fromage: Choisir, reconnaître, goûter 1200 fromages du monde.* Paris, France: Hachette Livre.

Carroll, Ricky. 2002. *Home Cheesemaking: Recipes for 75 Homemade Cheeses.* New Adams, MA: Storey Publishing.

Eekhof-Stork, Nancy. 1976. *The World Atlas of Cheese.* London, England: Paddington Press Ltd.

Ganugi, Gabriella. 2004. *Cheese: An Italian Pantry.* South San Francisco, CA: The Wine Appreciation Guild.

Harbutt, Juliet. 2002. *Cheese: A Comprehensive Guide to Cheeses of the World.* New York, NY: Lorenz Books.

Hooper, Allison. 2009. *In a Cheesemaker's Kitchen.* Websterville, VT: Vermont Butter & Cheese Co.

Masui, Kazuko, and Tomoko Yamada. 1996. *French Cheese.* London, England: Dorling Kindersley Publishing.

McCalman, Max, and David Gibbons. 2000. *The Cheese Plate.* New York, NY: Clarkson Potter.

Parr, Tami. 2009. *Artisan Cheese of the Pacific Northwest.* Woodstock, VT: Countryman Press.

Werlin, Laura. 2007. *Laura Werlin's Cheese Essentials: An Insider's Guide to Buying and Storing Cheese.* New York, NY: Stewart, Tabori, and Chang.

West Coast Cheese by Type

BLOOMY RIND

Adelle
Belora
Bucheret
Camellia
Cirrus
Euchre Mountain
French Prairie
Full Moon
Herbs in Bloom
Legato
Mt. Tam
Nocturne
Rouge et Noir Brie
Rouge et Noir Marin French Gold
Rouge et Noir Melange
Rouge et Noir Yellow Buck Chevre
Seastack
Siletz River Drum
Siletz River Stone
Silt Coos
St. Pat
Subblime
Sunset Bay
Valentine
Valsetz
White Rose
Yaquina Bay Pavé

BLUE

Caveman Blue
Crater Lake Blue
Creamy Bleu
Echo Mountain
Emerald City Blue
Fresh with Ewe Hint of Blue
Little Boy Blue
Oregon Blue
Oregonzola
Partly Sunny
Point Reyes Original Blue
Rogue River Blue
Rouge et Noir Marin Chevre Blue
Saggio
Smokey Blue
Two-Faced Blue
Wynoochee River Blue

FRESH

Burrata
Cabecou
chèvre
Clabbered Cottage Cheese
cream cheese
crème fraîche
Delice de la Vallee
Farm House
fromage blanc
Grande Rosa
Harvest
mascarpone
Monet Torte
Mozzarella
Mozzarella di Bufala
Oaxaca
Paneer
Panela
quark
queso fresco
requesón
ricotta
Rouge et Noir Breakfast Cheese
Spring/Summer Crottin
Thor's Special Crottin
Up in Smoke
Willapa White

HARD

Brindisi
Capricious
Dry Monterey Jack
Extra Mature Bandage Wrapped Cheddar
Impromptu

Mezzo Secco
Old World Portuguese
Oro Secco
Parmesan, Golden Glen Creamery
Parmesan, Gothberg Farms
Parmesan, Pine Stump Farms
Pecorino
Pine Stump Farms Asiago
Pozo Tomme
Queso de Oveja
Redmondo
Rosa
Serena
Super Aged Gouda
Tin Willow Tomme
Vella Dry Jack

SEMI-FIRM

Aged Raw Cheddar
Aged Tomme
Ashed Tomette
Ash Tomme
Asiago, Vella Cheese Company
Astraea
Baserri
Bea Truffled
Beer Cheese
Black Butte
Black Creek Buttery
Black Sheep Tomme
Blondie's Best
Boerenkaas
Boviago
Bovoncino
Broncha
Bubbly Cow
Cabralinda
Cabrero
Capraphilly
Capriago
Caprino Romano
Caproncino
Carmela
Carmody
Carmody Reserve
Causse Noir
Cecilia
Certoux
Chaparral
Cheddar
Cheddar in the Raw
Chevito
Cinco Esquinas
Classic
Classico
Cougar Gold
Crofter's Sward
Curado
Cylas
Daisy Raw Milk Cheddar
Dominoes
El Dorado Gold
Elk Mountain
Emaldi
Estero Gold
Farmhouse Cheddar
Flagsheep
Flagship
Flagship Reserve
Goat Manchego
Goat Tomme
Hannah Bridge
Hillis Peak
Ilahee Tomme
Jeddar
Killeen
La Panza Gold
Leaf-Wrapped Dominoes
Lionza
Marco Polo
Medium Cheddar
Medium Gouda
Mild Gouda
Montasio
Mont Blanchard
Mopsy's Best
Mountain Tomme
Mutschli, Pleasant Valley Dairy
Mutschli, Rosecrest Farm
Nocciola
Northern Gold
No Woman
Old Appletree Tomme
Organic Dry Jack
Pepato
Pleasant Valley
Port Edison
Redwood Log
Rio Santiam
River Cheddar
Romanello
Rosa Rugosa
Saint Olga
San Andreas
San Joaquin Gold
Sauveterre
Scio Heritage
Serenita
Shamrock Bouchon
Sharp Gouda
Shepherd
Shepherd's Gem
Sierra Mountain Tomme
Silver Mountain Aged Clothbound Cheddar
Skagit Parmesan
Smoked Flagship
St. George
Stout Cow
Swiss
Tipsy Cow
Tome du Corbier
Tomme de Sawtell
Trailhead
Tulare Cannonball
Tumalo Tomme
Two Rock Valley Cheese
Vache de Vashon
Valentina
Viking
Vineyard Tomme
Vintage Bandage Wrapped Cheddar
Weebles

SEMI-SOFT

Black Jewels
Caerphilly
Cascadia
Cayuse Mountain Goat
Che Vin
Chubut
Covered Bridge
Creamy Cheese
Crescenza
curds
Cynthian
Ewe-nique
Farmer's Cheese
Farmstead Gouda
Feta
Franklin's Rinconada Teleme
Franklin's Teleme
Goat Gouda
Gouda
Grisdale Goat
Guapier
Havarti
Italian Style Table Cheese
jack
Ladysmith
LaJersey
N. W. Comfort
Perrydale
Pondhopper
Renata

Sally Jackson Goat Cheese Wrapped in Grape Leaves
Sally Jackson Sheep Cheese Wrapped in Chestnut Leaves
Seascape
Spring Cheese
Sweet Dreams
Toma
UFO
Valley Doe
Valley Girl

SURFACE-RIPENED

Acapella
Bermuda Triangle
Blue Moon
Boho Bel
Buche, Juniper Grove Farm
Buche, Pug's Leap Farm
Cadenza
California Crottin
Cape Foulweather
Cardabella
Charolais
Crottin
Dafne
Dutchman's Flat
Eclipse
Figaro
Fog Lights
Humboldt Fog
Humbug Mountain
Hyku
Inverness
Kiku
Largo
Larkhaven Autumn Goatling
Larzac
Le Roi
Mary's Peak
Mejean
Mélange
Metronome
Minuet
Otentique
Pave, Andante Dairy
Pave, Pug's Leap
Pearl
Picolo
Pyramid
Rondo
Saint Helens
Sumi
Taupinière
Truffle Tremor

WASHED RIND

Bo Poisse
Brewleggio
Caldwell Crik Chevrette
Cascadian Frechette
Gravenstein Gold
Jupiter Moon
Larkhaven Goatling
Mayor of Nye Beach
Naughty Nellie
Opal Creek
Red Darla
Red Hawk
Rouge et Noir Schloss
Rouge et Noir Schlosskranz
Rouge et Noir Schlosskranz-Herz
Rousette
Silly Billy
Tomme de Cuivree
Wimer Winter

Index

Numbers in **boldface** indicate pages with illustrations or photographs.

Acapella, 59
Achadinha Cheese Company, **44,** 70, 77, 111
Adelle, 57
affinage, 26, 28, 57, 213
Aged Raw Cheddar, 88
Aged Tomme, 50
Alpine Lakes Sheep Cheese, 63, 96, 146
Alpines, **17, 40**
Alsea Acre Goat Cheese, 111, 118
Ancient Heritage Dairy, 57, 112, 126, 154, 160, 175, 182, 200
Andante Dairy, **34,** 90
  Acapella, 59
  Crottin, 99
  Figaro, 113
  Impromptu, 130
  Largo, 136
  Legato, 138
  Melange, 143
  Minuet, 144
  Nocturne, 151
  Pianoforte, 163
Animal Welfare Approved, 21, 81, 192
Antigo, 94
Appel Farms, 86, 101, 112, 118, 122, 168
Ashed Tomette, 61
Ash Tomme, 60
Asiago, 31, 33, 61, 164
Astraea, **48,** 62
Ayrshires, **17**

Barinaga, Marcia, 62
Barinaga Ranch, 62
Baserri, 62
Battro, Mariano, 91, 92
Bea Truffled, 200
Beecher's Handmade Cheese, 101, 114–115, 118, 132
Beer Cheese, 63
Belfiore Cheese Company, 112, 141, 147, 173
Bellwether Farms, 80, 97, 98, 118, 161, 173, 181
Belora, 63
Bermuda Triangle, 64
Black Butte, 64
Black Creek Buttery, 65, 87
Black Jewels, **33,** 65
Black Sheep Creamery, 66, 146, 160, 169, 173
Black Sheep Tomme, 66, 169
Blondie's Best, 66
bloomy rind cheese, 29, 49
blue cheese, 32, 49
Blue Moon, **48,** 67
Blue Rose Dairy, 33, 65, 90, 112, 124, 152
Bodega Artisan Cheese, 13, **41,** 85, 96, 112, 118, 120, 121, 173
Bodega Goat Cheese, 74, 169
Boerenkaas, **36,** 67
Bohemian Creamery, **34,** 68, 69, 77, 78
Boho Bel, 68
Bo Poisse, 68

Boviago, 69
Bovoncino, 69
Bravo Farms, **33,** 86, 87, 122, 132, 187, 196
Brevibacterium linens, 30, 170
Brewleggio, 69
Brindisi, 57, 70
Broncha, 70
Brown Swiss, **16**
Bryant, Cary, 95
Bubalus Bubalis, 147, 148
Bubbly Cow, 66
Buche, Juniper Grove Farm, 71
Buche, Pug's Leap Farm, 71
Bucheret, 72
Burrata, 57, 72

Cabecou, 73, 99
Cabralinda, 73
Cabrero, 74
Cadenza, 143
Caerphilly, 74
Caldwell, Gianaclis, 107, 165, 204
Caldwell, Vern, 165
Caldwell Crik Chevrette, **30, 33,** 57, 75
California Crottin, 52, 57, 75, 100
Camellia, 76
Cape Foulweather, 140
Capraphilly, 76
Capriago, **34,** 69, 77
Capricious, **44,** 77
Capricorns, 94
Caprino Romano, 78
Caproncino, 78
Cardabella, 79
Carmela, 80
Carmody, 80
Carmody Reserve, 80
Cascadia, 81
Cascadian Frechette, 81
Causse Noir, 82
Caveman Blue, 82
Cayuse Mountain Goat, **33,** 83
Cecilia, 83
Central Coast Creamery, **48,** 109, 119, 122, 183
Certified Humane Raised and Handled, 21, 72, 75, 76, 125
Certified Organic, 21
  Cowgirl Creamery, 93, 131, 149, 156, 163, 170, 190
  Fraga Farm, 110, 173
  Samish Bay Cheese Company, 134, 145, 167
  Spring Hill Cheese Company, 154
  Rosecrest Farms, 192
Certoux, 84
Chaparral, 84
Charolais, 85
Cheddar, **31,** 85–88
cheddaring, **38–39,** 65, 85
Cheddar in the Raw, 88
Che Vin, 89
Chevito, 89
chèvre, 25, **28, 42,** 90–91
Chubut, 91
Cinco Esquinas, 92
Cirrus, 29, 36–**37,** 92
Clabbered Cottage Cheese, 93
Classic, 93
Classico, 94
coagulant, 15, 22–24, 25, 57, 60
coagulation, 22–23, 72, 214
components, 15, 19
confinement, 20
Cougar Gold, 57, 94
Covered Bridge, 95
Cowgirl Creamery, 10, 97, 118
  Clabbered Cottage Cheese, 93
  Inverness, 131
  Mt. Tam, **41,** 149
  Paneer, 156
  Pierce Point, 163
  Red Hawk, 170
  St. Pat, 190
Crater Lake Blue, **33,** 95
cream cheese, 96
creamery, 19–20, 57
Creamy Bleu, 57, 96
Creamy Cheese, 97
crème fraîche, 97
Crescenza, 98
Crofter's Sward, 98
Crottin, **29,** 30, 75, 99–100
  Andante Dairy, 99
  Laura Chenel's Chevre, 99
  Mystery Bay Farm, 99, 100
  Pine Stump Farms, 100
cultures, 15, 21–22, 25, 67, 214
Cunnie, Maureen, 10
Curado, 101
curds, 22, 25–26, 101
Cylas, 102
Cynthian, 192
Cypress Grove Chevre, 10, 13, 64, 90, 115, 118, 129, 196

Dafne, 103
Daisy Raw Milk Cheddar, 88
Davis, Sheana, 103
Dee Creek Farm, 76, 89, 90, 102, 112
Delice de la Vallee, 103
Dominoes, 104, 170
Dry Jack, 104–105
Dry Monterey Jack, 105
Dutchman's Flat, 105

East Friesians, **18**
Echo Mountain, 106
Eclipse, 106
El Dorado Gold, 57, 107
Elk Mountain, 31, 107
El Michoacano, 97, 153, 157, 169, 173
Emaldi, 62
Emerald City Blue, 108
Estero Gold, 108
Estrella, Kelli, 83, 104, 134, 158
Estrella Family Creamery, 158
  Bea Truffled, 200
  Black Creek Buttery, 65, 87
  Brewleggio, 69
  Caldwell Crik Chevrette, **33,** 75
  Cecilia, 83
  Dominoes, 104
  Grisdale Goat, 125

Guapier, **40,** 126
Killeen, 134
Leaf Wrapped Dominoes, 104
Old Appletree Tomme, 153
Partly Sunny, **33,** 159
Red Darla, 170
Subblime, **33,** 190
Valentina, 200
Vineyard Tomme, 153
Weebles, **34, 48,** 203
Wynoochee River Blue, 205
Euchre Mountain, 205
Ewe-nique, 109
Extra Mature Bandage Wrapped Cheddar, 87

Fairview Farm, 81, 192
Farmer's Cheese, 109, 171
Farm House, 110
Farmhouse Cheddar, 88, 110
farmstead, 19–20, 57
Farmstead Gouda, 111
Fenacho, 94
Ferns' Edge Goat Dairy, 90
Feta, 111–113
Figaro, 113
Fiscalini, John, 139, 181
Fiscalini Farmstead Cheese Company, **34, 38–39,** 86, 87, 139, 147, 181
Flagsheep, 114
Flagship, 114–115
Flagship Reserve, 114–115
Fog Lights, 115
Food Alliance Sustainable Producer, 21, 95, 106, 155, 174, 188
Fraga Farm, 90, 110, 112, 173
Franklin's Rinconada Teleme, 116
Franklin's Teleme, 116
French Prairie, **48,** 117
fresh cheese, 28, 49, 53, 57
Fresh with Ewe Hint of Blue, 117
fromage blanc, 29, 118
Full Moon, 119
Geotrichum, 30
Gioia Cheese Company, 72, 141, 148, 173
Goat Gouda, **48,** 119
Goat Manchego, **41,** 121
Goat's Leap, 80, 103, 106, 129, 132, 191
Goat Tomme, 121
Golden Glen Creamery, 88, 102, 112, 122, 148, 157, 188
Goldin, Carine, 195
Goldin Artisan Goat Cheese, 81, 84, 194, 195
Gonzalez, Mariano, **38,** 139, 181
Gothberg, Rhonda, 74
Gothberg Farms, 74, 78, 88, 90, 112, 122, 157, 173
Gottreich, Lisa, 69
Gouda, 122–123
Pleasant Valley Dairy, 111, 123
Winchester Cheese Company, 123, 124
Grace Harbor Farms, 90
Grande Rosa, 124
Gravenstein Gold, 125
Gremmels, David, 95
Grisdale Goat, 125
Guapier, **30, 36,** 31, 126
Guernseys, **17**

haloir, 73, 214
Hannah Bridge, 126
hard cheese, 31, 49
Harley, Dee, 145
Harley Farms, 90, 112, 145, 173
Harvest, 127
Havarti, 127
Heart's Desire, 162
Herbs in Bloom, 128
Hillis Peak, 128
Holsteins, **16**
hooping, 26, 214
Humboldt Fog, **29,** 115, 129
Humbug Mountain, 140
Hyku, 129
Ilahee Tomme, 62, 130
Impromptu, 130
Inverness, 30, 52, 57, 131
Italian Style Table Cheese, **33,** 131

jack, 31, 132
Jackson, Sally, 180
Jacobs Creamery, 96, 141, 173
Jeddar, 88
Jerseys, **17**
Juniper Grove Farm, 90, 112, 118
Buche, 71
Dutchman's Flat, 105
Farmer's Cheese, 109
Otentique, **48,** 156
Pyramid, 168
Redmondo, 171
Thor's Special Crottin, 99
Tumalo Tomme, 197
Jupiter Moon, **42,** 57, 133

Karlin, Patty, 120
Keehn, Mary, 64, 129
Kendall Farms, 97
Kiku, 133
Killeen, 134
Kolisch, Pierre, 156, 168, 171
Kosher, 21, 72, 75, 76, 103, 125

La Clarine Farm, 107, 178, 186
lactation, 15, 214
lactose, 214
Ladysmith, 134
LaJersey, 135
LaManchas, **17**
La Mariposa, 91, 92
La Panza Gold, 135
Largo, 136
Larkhaven Autumn Goatling, 136
Larkhaven Farmstead Cheese, **33,** 83, 112,136, 137, 175, 185
Larkhaven Goatling, 137

Larzac, **45,** 137
Lacaunes, **18**
Laura Chenel's Chevre, 13, 73, 90, 99, 121, 193
Leaf-Wrapped Dominoes, 104
Legato, 30, 138
Le Roi, 138
Lionza, 139
Little Boy Blue, **32,** 140
Loleta Cheese Factory, 86, 127, 132

Marco Polo, 115
Marin French Cheese Company, 13, **36,** 168, 176, 177, 178
Mary's Peak, 140
mascarpone, 141
Matos, Joe, 154, 189
Matos, Mary, 189
Matos Cheese Factory, 11, **34–35, 40,** 189
Mayor of Nye Beach, 141
Medium Cheddar, 88
Medium Gouda, 124
Mild Gouda, 124
Mejean, 143
Mélange, 143
Metronome, 143
Meyenberg Goat Milk Products, 86, 96
Mezzo Secco, 31, 144
Midcoast Cheese Company, 116
milling, **39,** 65, 85–86
Minuet, 144
Monet Torte, 145
Montasio, 145
Mont Blanchard, 88
Monteillet, Joan, **45,** 79, 82
Monteillet, Pierre-Louis, **45,** 79
Monteillet Fromagerie, **45,** 79, 90, 137, 138, 143, 182
Mopsy's Best, 146
Morford, Patricia, 140, 142
Mountain Tomme, 146
Mount Townsend Creamery, 36–**37,** 92, 183, 195
Mozzarella, 28, 72, 147–148, 153
Mozzarella di Bufala, 148
Mt. Tam, 10, 29, **41,** 149, 170
Mutschli, Pleasant Valley Dairy, 149
Mutschli, Rosecrest Farm, 150
Mystery Bay Farm, 91, 99

Naughty Nellie, 150
New Moon Goat Dairy, 91
Nicolau Farms, 73, 91
Nigerian Dwarf, 165
Nocciola, 151
Nocturne, 151
Northern Gold, 64, 152
North Valley Farms Chevre, 91, 112
No Woman, 115
Nubians, **17**
N. W. Comfort, 152

Oakdale Cheese, 123
Oaxaca, 153
Ochoa Cheese Factory, 153, 169
Old Appletree Tomme, 153
Old World Portuguese, 31, 154
Opal Creek, 154
Oregon Blue, 32, 155, 174, 188
Oregonzola, **46–47,** 155
Organic Dry Jack, 105
Oro Secco, 144
Otentique, **48,** 156

Paneer, 156
Panela, 157
Parmesan, 157
Partly Sunny, **33,** 159
pasta filata, 147, 153, 203
paste, 28, 214
pasteurization, 24, 214
pasture-based, 20, 214
Pave, Andante Dairy, 143
Pave, Pug's Leap Farm, 159
Pearl, 160
Pecorino, 160
Pedrozo Dairy and Cheese Company, 64, 66, 152
Peluso, Franklin, 116
Penicillium candidum, 29, 214
Penicillium glaucom, 32
Penicillium roqueforti, 32
Pepato, 161
Perrydale, 161
Petit Bonheur, 162
Petit Marcel, 162
Phillips, Steve, 67, 203
Pholia Farm, 95, 107, 128, 164, 165, 204
Pianoforte, 163
Picolo, 136
Pierce Point, 163
Pine Stump Farms, 100, 127, 157, 164
Pine Stump Farms Asiago, 164
Pleasant Valley, 164
Pleasant Valley Dairy, 14, 111, 123, 149
Point Reyes Original Blue, 32, 166
Point Reyes Farmstead Cheese Company, 166
Pondhopper, 166
Port Edison, 167
Port Madison Farm, 91
  Beer Cheese, 63
  Blue Moon, **48,** 67
  Emerald City Blue, 108
  Farmhouse Cheddar, 88, 110
  Ripened Chevre, **48,** 100
  Saint Helens, **48,** 179
  Spring Cheese, 189
  White Rose, 203
Pozo Tomme, 167
Pug's Leap Farm, 60, 71, 159, 162
Pyramid, 168

Quail Croft Farmstead Cheese, 91, 98
quark, 168
Queseria Bendita, 169, 173

Queso de Oveja, 169
queso fresco, 29, 169
Quillisascut Cheese Company, **48,** 60, 101, 198

raw milk cheese, 24, 214
Red Darla, 170
Red Hawk, 10, 30, 170
Redmondo, 171
Redwood Hill Farm, 13, 72, 75, 76, 86, 91, 100, 112, 125
Redwood Log, 171
Renata, 172
rennet. *See* coagulant
requesón, 172–173
ricotta, 172–173
Rinconada Dairy, **40,** 84, 116, 135, 167
Rio Santiam, 173
Ripened Chevre, **48,** 100
River Cheddar, 88
Rivers Edge Chèvre, **40, 42,** 91, 142
  Astraea, 62
  Cape Foulweather, 140
  Euchre Mountain, 205
  Full Moon, 119
  Harvest, 127
  Heart's Desire, 162
  Humbug Mountain, 140
  Illahee Tomme, 130
  Jupiter Moon, **42,** 133
  Mary's Peak, 140
  Mayor of Nye Beach, 141
  Petit Bonheur, 162
  Saint Olga, **42,** 179
  Siletz River Drum, 186
  Siletz River Stone, 186
  Silt Coos, 119
  Spring/Summer Crottin, **48,** 100
  Sunset Bay, **43,** 191
  Up in Smoke, **33,** 199
  Valsetz, 202
  Yaquina Bay Pave, 205
River Valley Cheese, 91, 113, 148, 150, 173, 187, 201
Rogue Creamery, 10, 14, 87, 102
  Caveman Blue, 82
  Crater Lake Blue, **33,** 95
  Echo Mountain Blue, 106
  Oregon Blue, 155
  Oregonzola, **46–47,** 155
  Rogue River Blue, 174
  Smokey Blue, 188
Rogue River Blue, 10, **32,** 174
Romanello, 174
Rondo, 143
Rosa, 175
Rosa Rugosa, 175
Rosecrest Farm, 150, 192
Rouge et Noir
  Breakfast Cheese, 176
  Brie, 176
  Marin Chevre Blue, 178
  Marin French Blue, 177
  Marin French Gold, 177
  Melange, 178
  Schloss, 177
  Schlosskranz, 177
  Schlosskranz-Herz, 177
  Yellow Buck Chevre, 178
Rousette, 178
Rumiano Cheese Company, 13, 87, 102, 105, 132

Saanen, **17**
Saggio, 197
Saint Helens, **48,** 179
Saint Olga, **42,** 179
Sally Jackson Cheeses, 14, 172, 180
Sally Jackson Goat Cheese Wrapped in Grape Leaves, 180
Sally Jackson Sheep Cheese Wrapped in Chestnut Leaves, 180
Salmon, Javier, 185
salt, 15, 21–22, 26, **46**
Samish Bay Cheese Company, 88, 102, 113, 123, 134, 145, 148, 167, 169
San Andreas, 161, 181
San Joaquin Gold, **34,** 181
Sauveterre, 182
Scanlan, Soyoung, 57, 130
Scio Heritage, 57, 182
Sea Breeze Farm, **36,** 199
Seascape, 183
seasonal, 18, 214
Seastack, 36–**37,** 183
semi-firm cheese, 31, 49
semi-soft cheese, 30, 49
Serena, 184
Serenita, 184
Shamrock Artisan Goat Cheese, 61, 91, 171, 194
Shamrock Bouchon, 171
Sharp Gouda, 124
Shepherd, 185
Shepherd's Gem, 185
Sierra Mountain Tomme, 186
Sierra Nevada Cheese Company, 87, 91, 96, 113, 132
Siletz River Drum, 186
Siletz River Stone, 186
Silly Billy, 187
Silt Coos, 119
Silver Falls Creamery, 91
Silver Mountain Aged Clothbound Cheddar, 87, 187
Silver Springs Creamery, 88, 93, 97, 135
Siskiyou Crest Goat Dairy, 91, 113
Skagit Parmesan, 188
Smoked Flagship, 115
Smokey Blue, 188
Spring Cheese, 189
Spring Hill Cheese Company, 87, 102, 105, 113, 132, 154, 168
Spring/Summer Crottin, **48,** 100
St. George, 11, 189
St. Pat, 190
Steamboat Island Goat Farm, 88, 113, 132
Stout Cow, 66
Subblime, **33,** 190

Sumi, 191
Sunset Bay, **43,** 191
Super Aged Gouda, 124
surface-ripened cheese, 29–30, 49
Sweet Dreams, 192
Swiss, 192

Taupinière, 193
Thor's Special Crottin, 99
Three Sisters Farmstead Cheese, 184
Tillamook County Creamery, 14, 87
Tin Willow Tomme, 66, 169
Tipsy Cow, 66
Toma, 193
tomme, 214
Tome du Corbier, 194
Tomme de Cuivree, 194
Tomme de Sawtell, 195
Trailhead, 195
Train, George, 14
triple cream, 29, 51, 136, 149, 170, 177, 214
Truffle Tremor, 196
Tulare Cannonball, 33, 196
Tumalo Farms, 94, 151, 166
Tumalo Tomme, 197
Two-Faced Blue, 32, 197
Two Rock Valley, 198
Two Rock Valley Cheese, **41,** 198
tyrosine crystals, 27, 82, 122, 124, 155, 182, 214

UFO, **48,** 198
unhooping, 26, 214
unpasteurized, *See* raw milk cheese
Up in Smoke, **33,** 199

Vache de Vashon, 199
Valentina, 200
Valentine, **36,** 200
Validus Certified Responsible Producer, 21, 139, 181
Valley Doe, 201
Valley Ford Cheese, 108
Valley Girl, 201
Valsetz, 202
Vella, Ignazio, 174
Vella, Tom, 155
Vella Cheese Company, 13, 14, 87, 132
  Asiago, **33,** 61
  Daisy Raw Milk Cheddar, 88
  Italian Style Table Cheese, 131
  Mezzo Secco, 144
  Romanello, 174
  Toma, 193
  Vella Dry Jack, 104–105
Viejo, 101
Viking, 202
Vineyard Tomme, 153
Vintage Bandage Wrapped Cheddar, 88
Volbeda, Rod, 70

washed curd, 25, 214
washed rind cheese, 30, 49, 51, 57
Washington State University Creamery, 14, 87, 94, 202
Weebles, **34, 48,** 203
Wesselink, Jules, 124
whey, 25–26, 214
wheying off, 25, 214
White Rose, 203
Willamette Valley Cheese Company, **36, 48,** 67, 70, 87, 117, 127, 132, 161
Willapa Hills Farmstead Cheese, 117, 140, 197, 204
Willapa White, 204
Wimer Winter, 204
Winchester Cheese Company, 123, 124
Wynoochee River Blue, 205

Yaquina Bay Pavé, 205
Yerba Santa Goat Dairy, 89, 91, 185
yield, 18–19